the
Community
of the
SPIRIT

*To John C. Wenger, mentor
and longtime colleague.*

Foreword by
Alan Kreider

the Community of the SPIRIT

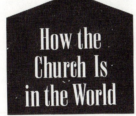

How the
Church Is
in the World

Revised Edition

C. Norman Kraus

HERALD PRESS
Scottdale, Pennsylvania
Waterloo, Ontario

Library of Congress Cataloging-in-Publication Data
Kraus, C. Norman (Clyde Norman), 1924-
    The community of the Spirit : how the church is in the world /
C. Norman Krause.—Rev. ed.
        p. cm.
    Includes bibliographical references and index.
    ISBN 0-8361-3619-5 (alk. paper)
    1. Church. I. Title.
BV600.2.K68 1993
262—dc20   92-34740
                                                                  CIP

All Bible quotations are used by permission, all rights reserved,
and unless otherwise indicated are from the *Revised Standard
Version of the Bible*, copyright 1946, 1952, 1971 by the Division of
Christian Education of the National Council of the Churches of
Christ in the USA. Excerpts marked (NRSV) are from the *New
Revised Standard Version Bible,* copyright 1989, by the Division of
Christian Education of the National Council of the Churches of
Christ in the USA; (NEB) from *The New English Bible*. © The
Delegates of the Oxford University Press and the Syndics of the
Cambridge University Press 1961, 1970.

THE COVER is based on the Mennonite World Conference
(MWC) logo designed by Glen Fretz for MWC Assembly 11, held
in Strasbourg, France, in 1984. Used by permission of Mennonite
World Conference, 7 avenue de la Forêt-Noire, 67000 Strasbourg,
France.

THE COMMUNITY OF THE SPIRIT
Copyright © 1993 by Herald Press, Scottdale, Pa. 15683
    Published simultaneously in Canada by Herald Press,
    Waterloo, Ont. N2L 6H7. All rights reserved
Library of Congress Catalog Number: 92-34740
International Standard Book Number: 0-8361-3619-5
Printed in the United States of America
Cover and book design by Paula M. Johnson

1 2 3 4 5 6 7 8 9 10 00 99 98 97 96 95 94 93

Contents

Foreword

Missionaries, the apostle remarked in a famous passage (2 Cor. 5:16-20) are "ambassadors for Christ." Their ambassadorial tasks include formulating a message ("the message of reconciliation") and conveying it through persuasion and entreaty. But good ambassadors also develop imaginative empathy and good listening. They learn a perceptive detachment enabling them to discern the unspoken (and often unrecognized) assumptions of the people to whom they are sent. If they do this well, if they "regard no one from a human point of view," they convey a message people can understand. Their message is "news," for it speaks to the real circumstances of the hearers.

C. Norman Kraus is a missionary theologian. His major recent writings (*Jesus Christ Our Lord* and *God Our Savior*) have been enriched by his encounter with the people and civilization of Japan. But *The Community of the Spirit*, which I am pleased to welcome in this revised edition, has emerged from his missionary encounter with North America. Here is a learned and lucid restatement of the Christian message that grows out of Kraus' sensitive, ambassadorial listening the leitmotif of modern North American life—individualism.

Sociologists have recently been giving individualism serious attention. According to Robert Bellah and his co-researchers in *Habits of the Heart*, individualism is the most habitual of North American habits. "Individualism," they remark, "has marched inexorably through our history." Although they are not unremitting critics of individualism, they fear it "may have grown cancerous." To change the metaphor, the very air modern North Americans breathe, which may seriously damage their health, is individualism.

To Christians of this individualistic civilization, Kraus offers good news. Kraus knows how to do this because he has been attentive to North America and its Christians. Is it because he is a slightly alien American, a Mennonite who came to maturity in the years following World War II, that his perceptions are so acute? Kraus also communicates well with North American readers. He knows their institutions and assumptions. And as a historical theologian he is a recognized authority on their ways of thinking about God. To them he offers not a pious ratification of North American approaches to faith but an alternative message that is both comprehensible and converting.

God's means of working throughout history, Kraus is convinced, is the building of community. God takes individuals, such as Abraham and Sarah, with utmost seriousness. God cherishes individuality. But instead of individualism, God's design for individuals is life within committed, covenanted relationships. It is Jesus, upon whose person and work Kraus repeatedly reflects, who shows with finality God's desire that individuals live in community. And Jesus, through his life, death, and resurrection, inaugurated the age of the Spirit, in which relationships are restored and structured according to God's original intention.

As Kraus thinks with the reader, familiar biblical words take on deeper meaning. Covenant, *shalom, agape, koinonia*—Kraus discusses each comprehensibly, at times grippingly, viewing them as the social substance of the gospel. Jesus' disciples can't make it on their own. As they discover the dynamism encoded in these words, they realize why "the reality of the new community [is] a part of the proclamation." It is from self-sufficiency, and for shalom-filled common life, that Jesus saves North Americans.

And not only North Americans. Writing in England, I am aware that the liberation from the sin of narcissism is as desperately needed in Europe. Three-quarters of our human family struggles in squalor. Meanwhile, our errant northern civilization busily constructs a Babel of perpetually dissatisfied, eco-destructive self-aggrandizement. What defiance of the way of community this represents!

But God is doing something new. One of my delights is to find people throughout the world who, through the work of God's Spirit, have been liberated to live the Jesus way—imaginatively, interdependently, humbly, attractively. For such people, this book will be an invaluable resource. For congregations and small groups, Kraus' arguments will provide springboards to dive into fruitful discussion. And for all who name Jesus as Lord but are inhaling the polluted air of consumptive individualism, *The Community of the Spirit* may be a means by which our missionary God gives them a second wind.

—*Alan Kreider*
Manchester, England

Author's Preface

It has been two decades since I wrote the first edition of *The Community of the Spirit*. Much has happened in the meantime, so it was necessary to do more than simply reedit the original. The present volume is not only a revision but an update and expansion of the first edition. While there is considerable new material included, I have not altered the basic view or subject matter.

Specifically, I have added a new chapter on "Jesus and the Church," and a revised chapter on "Biblical Perspectives on the Individual-in-Community"(which first appeared in *The Authentic Witness*). Beside these additions I have freely added paragraphs and sections to the existing chapters, and a bibliography and index are provided.

Since the early 1970s the church growth movement has emphasized the importance of the church as an expression of the kingdom of God. "Holistic mission" has become almost a shibboleth. The charismatic movement has focused on renewal and congregational expression of the gifts of the Spirit. However, one still does not find much emphasis in evangelical Christianity on the church/congregation itself as a community of witness.

A number of Roman Catholic biblical scholars like Raymond Brown and Rudolph Schnackenburg have added significantly to the literature on the biblical theology of the church and its place in the world. At the same time, the Protestant ecumenical movement has turned its attention away from a church-centered theological approach—a trend that was already beginning in the 1970s.

Outside the church, the New Age movement has made a nebulous but significant impact on the piety and beliefs of many Christians. The appeal of individualism, relativism, and the focus on self-improvement continue to impact our concepts of spirituality. The popularity of nonreligious communalism, which flourished in the sixties and seventies, has diminished. Nevertheless, there seems to be a yearning for relationships which can give meaning to life among the so-called "baby boomer" generation, as many of them return to the church.

I hope this biblically based study of community in Christian life and mission will challenge those who view "church" only as a place to attend for personal inspiration. And for those seeking to live out the gospel in intentional communities, may it offer encouragement and support.

—*C. Norman Kraus*
Harrisonburg, Virginia

1

Pentecost and the Gospel

The formation of the community of the Spirit at Pentecost in 30 C.E. is part of the Christian gospel. For many years now we have been told that the gospel, or good news, is about the events which fulfilled the promises God gave through the prophets to Israel. The rather quaint King James phrase "and it came to pass" puts it well. The gospel actually happened. Jesus of Nazareth came as the promised Messiah and by his resurrection from the dead was "declared to be Son of God with power according to the [Holy] Spirit" (Rom. 1:3-4, NRSV alternate reading).

Not said with equal clarity and conviction has been that the events of that first Christian Pentecost were part of this incarnation drama. The word *gospel* has come to have distinctly religious connotations. People don't call receiving the good news of a raise in salary or long-awaited vacation "gospel." These are nonreligious events belonging to everyday life, which we refer to as *secular* (from the Latin meaning "of this age"). However, at the time the New Testament was written the word we have translated gospel referred to just that kind of happening—for example, the coronation of a new king, or a victory in war.

On the day of Pentecost Peter told the crowds that it

was what Jesus had done publicly ("among you, as you yourselves know") during his ministry that had convinced them he was from God. *Gospel* is different from doctrine, exhortation, theory, or belief. It announces an event.[1]

The specific shape of the good news in the Christian tradition is the announcement that what was long promised and expected has now happened. Promise has become reality. That is the essential message of the New Testament. The good news is not that there is more to come *in the future*. It is not the announcement of heaven by and by, or of a future earthly kingdom. It is not that if one believes hard enough, *faith will make it so*. It is not that the *correct philosophical formula* has been found to demonstrate that "God is there" after all. Neither is it that a *new ethical principle of agape love* has been given to free men and women from the tyranny of legalism.

The gospel is this: the promised "power of God for salvation" (Rom. 1:16) has become reality for all who have eyes to see and ears to hear![2] Of course, some still have not heard or will not hear the news. But the gospel proclaims a *present* reality. That is of the essence.

The gospel announces something which both happened in the past and is happening in the present. The story begins with what happened when Jesus the Messiah initiated a new chapter in the history of humanity. He came announcing that a new era in the rule of God was about to be inaugurated, and he himself initiated it in his ministry. But that happened many years ago; if it is truly good news for humankind in the twentieth century, then there must be something happening in the present tense also. *If what happened in the past is really part of the gospel, it must have a demonstrable relation to present reality.*

The relation of a past event to the present is, indeed, a crucial problem. The earliest Christians already faced it. After all, the past is past whether it be four days, forty years, or forty centuries. Yesterday is memory. Today is reality.

The days immediately following the crucifixion were some of the darkest! The disciples were in despair because all their experiences, all their present realities with Jesus, all their hopes for the future were suddenly a memory. When they learned that Jesus was alive on the third day, their hopes for the *future* were revived. Now he might yet bring in the rule (kingdom) he had announced. But what of the *present* reality? The only word from the risen Christ was "wait."

At first they found it difficult even to ask the question about the present. Their minds jumped to a future near or far when Jesus would restore the kingdom to Israel. But the good news he came preaching was that the promise is already a significant reality in the present time, not that fulfillment has become more certain though postponed to an unknown future.

What happened at Pentecost provided the connecting link between past and present. The continuity between the historical presence of Jesus and our present salvation was disclosed in the living presence of the Spirit of Christ. At Pentecost Christ became a dynamic contemporary reality—never again to be absent from his disciples.[3] As Martin Luther once put it, the Spirit is the true *vicar*, that is, the authoritative presence of

Christ. The Spirit is not some religious institutional representative who preserves Christ's legacy in his absence.

The genius of New Testament Christianity is that it interprets the gospel not merely as a legacy from the past nor a new certainty for future fulfillment. The good news is that the promise has been fulfilled; hope is realized. In a profound new way God's presence and power are a *now* reality to accomplish God's will on earth. This is not, of course, to deny a future culmination—but the problem has been that preoccupation with future reality has undercut present expectation and possibility.

The Meaning of Pentecost

Pentecost as reported in Acts is the climax of a three-act drama of incarnation. Act one presents various scenes in the ministry of Jesus. Act two is the passion of the Christ. Act three is the triumphant advance of the victorious Lord. At Pentecost "the promise of the Father" was fulfilled (Luke 24:49 and Acts 1:4).

The ministry, death, and resurrection were not the completion of the promise. That is why Jesus told his followers to wait in Jerusalem. Jerusalem was the point of departure for the triumphant mission, and the disciples were to "sit tight" (*kathisate*) until the promise had become reality (Luke 24:27-28).

It was not simply a matter of their receiving an individual spiritual capability for service and witness to what Christ had already finished. No, they were not to begin their mission until the Father had completed the formation of the new body through which the Christ would expand his presence and ministry.[4]

The drama of incarnation does not conclude with a final act that neatly wraps up the loose ends of the story and draws the curtain. Rather it points to an open future for those involved. Pentecost is a commencement in the same sense that we use the word to describe a graduation. It is simultaneously climax and beginning.[5] It concludes with the assurance that this is not the end but the beginning.

The Christ is not dead or absent in some far-off spiritual realm. His ministry is not concluded, but universalized through his new body (Baillie, 1948:145-46). The kingdom he announced has not been set aside until some future millennium but enters a new era of fulfillment with the pouring out of the Spirit. Surely this is part of the good news!

It is difficult to believe that Luke did not intentionally use parallel language when he spoke of the Spirit's work in preparing the human body of the historical Messiah and in preparing a new human body for the resurrected Lord. According to his account the angel told Mary, "the Holy Spirit *will come upon you*, and the *power* of the Most High will overshadow you. . ." (Luke 1:35, emphasis added). In Acts 1:8 Jesus told his disciples, "You shall receive *power* when the Holy Spirit *has come upon you*. . ." (emphasis added).

In both cases the body of Christ is formed through a special work of God's Spirit. This is obviously incarnational language. It strongly suggests the closest kind of association between the ministry of Jesus, which was in a unique way the work of the Spirit (Luke 3:22; 5:1, 18), and the ministry of the church. That the Christ is still present and at work among humankind in an earthly body is an integral part of the good news.

The continuity between the earthly ministry of Jesus and the mission of the apostles is also indicated by Luke in his report of the discussion between the resurrected Jesus and his disciples. The disciples continued to talk about "the kingdom of God" (Acts 1:3), but they still did not grasp the true nature of that rule which Jesus came to inaugurate. They still viewed it as the restoration of national autonomy to Israel under a political Messiah. They were still thinking of the kingdom in terms of political power.

Jesus brushed aside their misconceived questions about the "times and seasons." He spoke instead of the kingdom as the power of God at work among humankind in history. He associated the presence of the kingdom with the promised power of the Holy Spirit—which would be theirs to fulfill his mission.

This was the same word he had spoken during his pre-resurrection ministry. In Matthew 12:28, for example, he identified the presence of the rule of God with the power of the Holy Spirit which would come upon them. In other contexts he pointed to God's power to heal, to establish righteousness, and to accomplish his will on earth as signs or evidences of divine rule.

We conclude then that the gospel and salvation of which Jesus and his apostles spoke included the events of Pentecost. In these events the promise became a continuing reality. The mission which Jesus inaugurated in his earthly ministry was continued through the presence of his Spirit in his new body. This is indeed good news! (In chapter 3 we will exam-

ine more carefully the relation of Jesus' earthly ministry and the mission of the church.)

What Really Happened?

What *really* happened at Pentecost? This question now
becomes crucial, for Pentecost is part of the gospel.
The question has been asked and answered by many
commentators and theologians, but it has seldom been
asked in this context.

The answers have largely focused on the manifestations that caught the attention of the puzzled onlookers. Did the reported phenomena *literally* happen or
not? When asked this way, the question is put into a
twentieth-century, Western context. "Really" is interpreted as "literally" or "empirically."

What did the crowds see and hear? The questions
usually continue in the same vein: Should we expect a
literal recurrence of such manifestations in the church
today? What kind of psychological experience do individuals have when they receive the Spirit? Such questions are intriguing and may be important for some
purposes, but to make them central is to remain in the
company of the onlookers at Pentecost!

Luke himself makes clear what he understood to be
of central importance in the account. He does this both
by his choice of language and by the way he constructs
the account. His language alludes to parallels with the
birth, life, and ministry of Jesus, and to the story of the
Exodus of Israel. These allusions focus our attention
on the formation of a new people of God.[6]

He reinforces this focus with his summaries in 2:43-
47 and 4:32-27. Each summary highlights preceding

developments and acts as a bridge to the next sections of the story. The summaries, therefore, indicate clearly what Luke thought really happened at Pentecost. What really happened at Pentecost was *the formation of the new covenant community of the Spirit.* Let us examine more closely these characteristics of Luke's account.

The teaching that the church was born at Pentecost is, of course, not new. Neither is the idea that there is both continuity and discontinuity with Israel a new one. Luke's many allusions to Exodus underscore the parallelism between Israel's transformation from a "mixed multitude" into a new covenant people. It has not been sufficiently recognized that the new thing which happened on Pentecost was precisely *the new* community.

The immediate Pentecost manifestations of the Spirit's presence were fire, wind, and speaking in other tongues. All three have a rich and varied symbolic use in the Old Testament and other Jewish literature. As the Israelites left Egypt the special presence of Yahweh leading his people was manifested in the "pillar of fire" (Exod. 13:21-22; 14:24). Now that presence appears again and disperses itself, resting on each one in the representative new Israel (Acts 2:3).

The Pentecost imagery is of a central bonfire mysteriously dividing into individual tongues of fire resting on each head. This surely alludes to passages like Jeremiah 31:33-34 which foresees a time when the Word of God will no longer be merely an external law but put into every individual Israelite's heart.

At Pentecost the mysterious "violent wind" which dried up the waters of the Red Sea (Exod. 14:21) and whipped in the faces of the Israelites as they crossed to Sinai now again filled the house with a roar. Luke fully identifies this wind as God's Spirit.

The play on words in the original languages of the Bible makes this more obvious. Both *ruach* (Hebrew) and *pneuma* (Greek) have the double meaning of wind and spirit. There are other words for wind that do not have the double meaning. These words occur in the Septuagint account of the wind (*anemos*) drying up the Red Sea and also in the Acts 2 account of the rushing wind (*pnoe*) at Pentecost. But the original texts make it plain that the *anemos* of Exodus and the *pnoe* of Acts are in fact the *pneuma*, the wind/spirit, of God.

The Pentecost symbolism of speaking and hearing in different dialects is also complex. It most likely alludes to the confusion of languages at Babel (Gen. 11:7-9). The Spirit's presence now reverses Babel. As Paul said, in Christ there are no "barbarians"—those of uncouth languages (Col. 3:11). The breaking down of language barriers also indicates the universality of the salvation message and therefore the mission and nature of the new people being formed.

The connection of "speaking in tongues" with the Exodus and Sinai is not so apparent until we learn this: There was a Jewish tradition that the Mosaic Law had been given in seventy languages simultaneously. This symbolism indicated the universal scope of the Law's authority. Luke's account of the new covenant being announced in many languages may well parallel this Jewish tradition "about the marvelous manifestation of divine power that accompanied the giving of the law at Sinai."[7]

In his sermon, Peter explained all this as the fulfillment of Joel's prophecy. Jesus, the true Messiah, has sealed the new covenant in his death. Now risen and victorious, he is forming his new people. Just as the Israelites were "baptized into Moses . . . in the sea" (1 Cor. 10:2), marking decisively their separation from their old family identity in Egypt, so Peter called his audience to be baptized and save themselves from the old "corrupt generation" (*genea*).

Just as Israel received their new identity as the people of God at Sinai through the *gift of the Torah (Law)*, so the new people is constituted through the *gift of the Spirit*. And just as great signs accompanied Israel's deliverance and formation into a covenant nation, so "signs and wonders done through the apostles" accompanied the birth of the new community of the Spirit.

The Legacy of Evangelicalism

The interpretation of Pentecost which I have offered differs in several significant aspects from the usual Pentecostal or Fundamentalist interpretations. It will help us to see where the significant issues lie if we put what has been said into historical perspective. The "standard" interpretations offered in evangelicalism have been influenced by theological developments in the church as well as objective biblical interpretation.

Modern evangelicalism is heir of seventeenth-century Protestant orthodoxy. Orthodoxy focused its attention on the doctrines of an objective atonement and justification by faith in the "finished work of Christ." It also reacted against the vagaries of "spiritualism" and stressed Scripture as the touchstone for any claims to Spirit guidance or enlightenment.

Thus neither the Reformed nor Lutheran orthodoxy accentuated the gift of the Spirit and the implications of this gift for the life of the church. Because modern evangelicalism mostly accepted the basic assumptions and working definitions of this theological tradition, it has never come fully to grips with the significance of the gospel of Pentecost.

Let me explain. Contemporary American evangelicalism is broadly divided into three schools on the interpretation of Pentecost and the work of the Holy Spirit. Two of these, which I shall refer to as *pentecostal* and *pietistic*, stand in sharp contrast. The third position, which we may call *holiness*, developed within Pietism. Orthodoxy has been reluctantly tolerant of the holiness tradition in its Wesleyan and Keswick expressions but has been quite suspicious of Pentecostalism.

Pietism arose within Orthodoxy in the latter sixteenth and early seventeenth centuries. It was a renewal movement within the established Lutheran and Reformed churches. The Pietists were deeply concerned to correct the formalism, intellectualism, and lack of personal involvement in the established churches. This led them to stress individual piety and spiritual experience. They accepted the established Protestant institutions in which they were operating as valid churches, but, deploring the churches' lack of true spirituality, Pietists worked for individual renewal and authenticity.

This influenced pietist interpretation of the Pentecost experience. They viewed it as an experience of individual renewal (true conversion in contrast to profession) and preparation for holy living. They did not visualize its outcome as primarily a new corporate reality—a new body or church indwelled by the Holy Spirit.

Pietists accepted orthodoxy in word and sacrament as the authenticating mark of the visible church. Their pious "conventicles" were fellowships for mutual religious discipline which added warmth and spiritual depth to orthodoxy.[8] The notion that members of these "little churches within the church" were the "true church" was implicit, but it was not clearly expressed in their theology of the Spirit.

The precise character of the conventicle depended on the relative importance attached to *experience* of the Spirit's presence and power (feeling) or to *faith* as an act of the intellect and will. An emphasis on experience stimulated fellowship and an open expression of the Spirit's "gifts." An emphasis on faith tended to produce groups for the spiritual disciplines of Bible study, prayer, and moral living.

The seeds of future dissension and divisions lay in these different emphases on experience and faith. The Wesleyan wing of Pietism stressed the "felt Christ" (a term from Whitefield) and holiness.[9] Although Wesley fully acknowledged the Spirit's work in conversion, he placed more emphasis on the "second work" of sanctification and motivation for holy living. In time this emphasis on the special continuing work of the Holy Spirit opened the way for experiencing the "gifts" of the Spirit. These gifts were given to strengthen the individual's assurance and to lift everyday life to a higher plane.

In contrast to the holiness emphasis (which incidentally tended toward Arminian theological assumptions), the more orthodox (Calvinistic) Pietists insisted that the special gifts of the Spirit were strictly a New Testament phenomenon that ceased with the apostolic generation.[10] They were part of the initial revelation, like miracles and signs which the apostles performed to validate the message.

These pietistic evangelicals continued a modified Calvinistic position, maintaining the doctrines of salvation by God's election and the eternal security of believers. Evidence of election was given through an inner assurance and change of attitude, not by outward experiences. They insisted that believers received the Holy Spirit when they accepted Christ. The Spirit's filling was to be accepted by *faith* and not on the basis of some special experience or manifestation of gifts.

A third variant in American evangelicalism arose in the late nineteenth and early twentieth century and chose the name Pentecostalism.[11] This movement muted sanctification as the dominant work of the Spirit. It accentuated the ecstatic, emotional aspects of experience in a "baptism of the Spirit and fire." In a literal way it reintroduced the gifts of tongues, prophecy, healing, and other works of faith as signs of the Spirit's presence. The gift of tongues was the special sign of baptism by the Spirit. Implicitly the signs were seen also as the authenticating mark of the true church.

All three of these positions continue within evangelicalism. The differences are most pronounced in the rift between Pentecostalism and pietistic Fundamentalism. These differences have been obvious and in some cases explosive. Overlooked, however, have been the significant agreements and shared assumptions of the two movements. Both begin with the same individualistic definition of salvation. Both interpret Pentecost as incidental to a salvation based on the death and resurrection of Christ alone. Both view the infilling by the outpoured Spirit as the private experience of an aggregate of saved individuals. Pentecost is not an essential part of their gospel of salvation.

Neither the pentecostal nor pietistic wings of modern American evangelicalism have recognized the centrality of the community of the Spirit. Both have viewed the gift of the Spirit as essentially an individual experience. Pentecostals have accentuated the ecstatic manifestations as signs to the believer. Pietists have stressed the inner resources which the fullness of the Spirit provides for personal piety and witness.

Neither has seen that the fundamental work of the Spirit at Pentecost was the *formation of the new community itself.* Perhaps a new perspective on the central meaning of Pentecost is needed to help us surmount and resolve the old conflict created in part by the very inadequacy of categories used by both sides.

Community and Individual[12]

The interrelation of individual and community, and the new significance of the individual in the new covenant, are at the heart of what happened at Pentecost. The individual acquires a new prominence in the Pentecost story and in the New Testament as a whole. That the community of the Spirit is made up of "Spirit-filled" individuals is one genuinely new aspect. Indeed, the very notion of a community constituted by a "baptism of the Spirit"—in contrast to law—implies a new range and depth to individuality.

This new appreciation for and focus on the individual person is symbolized in the dispersion of the fire of God's presence into individual tongues of flame. And Peter's call to repent and be baptized is an appeal to individuals to change their allegiance. Crowds do not repent; individuals do.

The prophet Joel, whom Peter cites, had prophesied this surprising new personalizing of the gift of the Spirit across all class lines and distinctions. Jeremiah also foresaw the new covenant that would be written on each person's heart so everyone in the new peoplehood would share individually in the knowledge of the Lord (Jer. 31:31-34).

This new element of *Spirit* rather than *law* as the basis for community is significant. Luther's polarity of law and grace, which became the standard Protestant category for biblical interpretation, obscured this even more elemental polarity of Law and Spirit in Protestant interpretations of Pentecost. Thus the attention of Protestant theology has been diverted from the original import of this new disclosure of individual dignity and freedom in Christian community.[13]

The significance of the individual as manifested at Pentecost is not to be understood as an essentially private and theological justification by faith. The individual is not freed from institutional bondage under law to experience autonomy under grace. At Pentecost persons who were members of a community of law— "born under law" (Gal. 4:1-4)—were called to become

part of a new community of the Spirit. The fundamental difference between the old and new covenants
is the shift from Torah (law) to Spirit as the formative
basis of community. What is involved here, then, is primarily the relation of Law and Spirit, and only second-
arily of law and grace.

Law, Spirit, and the Individual

The significance of this becomes clearer when we examine the relation of law and individuality. Law is for
the regulation of societal activity and for the sake of the
group. By definition it subjects the individual to the
group to preserve the cohesiveness of the community.
As a regulatory social institution it must be stated as
nearly as possible in universal terms which can be uniformly applied and enforced.

Law by its very nature generalizes and inhibits individual expression in favor of the group. From the van-
tage point of individual development, therefore, the
best statute is one stated in the negative—which can be
uniformly interpreted, and enforced while leaving the
greatest scope for positive action. But where there is
no individual dynamic and motivation, even the best
law cannot bring about what it prescribes—or to pre-
vent what it prohibits, as Paul so clearly saw. The Spirit
overcomes this weakness of the Law.

To compensate for the Law's handicaps and to keep
the Jewish community intact, the scribal tradition (developed from the time of Ezra) expanded and concret-
ized the prescriptions of Torah. Pharisaism was one of
the highest types of legal religion and morality ever
achieved in the ancient world. It developed during a

period when the Jews commonly assumed that the Spirit of prophecy had been withdrawn. They had concluded that the religious community would have to be preserved by legal regulation and tradition. This Pharisaic community, with its comprehensive system of both prohibitive and prescriptive statutes, provides the background for understanding the New Testament account of Jesus and the rise of the church.

Jesus found himself in sharp conflict with the scribal tradition. In contrast to the scribes' legal authority, he was bearer and dispenser of the Spirit. He promised that the Spirit would lead his followers into all truth. While he respected and used the "law and the prophets," he did not construct a new religious system by developing their implications in some casuistical way.

For Jesus "the sabbath [law] was made for man and not man for the sabbath" (Mark 2:27). The "new commandment" Jesus left to his followers was not simply different in intention from the Mosaic covenant. It was new in kind (*kainē*). It was new precisely in the sense that it was not a legal statute. His community would be held together not by his new law but by his presence. In Pauline terms the community's bond of unity would be the Spirit (Eph. 4:3).

Our social definitions and presuppositions, inherited from the previous century, have largely blinded us to the reality and dynamics of this organic, spiritual community, which the New Testament calls *church*. The American denominational concept of church has followed the political model of John Locke's "social contract."[14] It has viewed the church as a voluntary society formed by a contractual arrangement (called "covenant" in religious terms) between individuals who share commitments and goals. As with Locke, the contract is voluntary, legal, and functions to preserve the freedom and equality of the individuals as much as the unity and identity of the group.[15] Thus we have failed to understand how the church can be the matrix for developing individuality and freedom in Christ.

Modern insights from anthropology, sociology, and psychology confirm the biblical presupposition that the basic human unit is not the independent individual before God but the *individual-in-community* before God. We become self-conscious individuals only in community relationships. Indeed, we might say that personhood is the gift of the familial community.

Thus community is integrally involved in the individuals' self-identity. The nature of their responsibility and freedom is defined by the nature of their community. When we view the formation of the community of the Spirit at Pentecost from this perspective, we appreciate its profound significance for the enhancement of individual spiritual attainment.

The Pentecostal Koinonia

The biblical concept of individual-in-community as the basic unit of personal existence dominates the account of the first Christian Pentecost. The setting is a religious festival where Jews of the dispersion have gathered to celebrate their national identity and cohesion. During the festival these celebrants are called to reject their allegiance to the old religious community and openly identify with a new Messianic community in which the main feature is the Holy Spirit's renewed presence with God's people. This is the meaning of "repent, and be baptized. . . . Save yourselves from this crooked generation" (Acts 2:38-40).

The story begins with the 120 disciples "all together in one place." When Peter is presented as spokesman, he is "standing with the eleven," and he appeals to the group to substantiate what he is saying. The crowd responds to "Peter and the rest of the apostles." Through repentance and baptism (Acts 2:37-42) they transfer identity and allegiance from the old to the new community of the "one hundred and twenty" disciples.

The account which follows accents the unity and fellowship of the new community. The new group is made up of forgiven individuals finding new identity in the koinonia of the Spirit. They are *individuals-in-koinonia*. It is precisely this new fellowship of the Spirit that so impresses "all the people."

On the day of Pentecost, to be saved meant to join the messianic (later called the Christian) community. On that day baptism in the name of Jesus Christ was a public act of acknowledging that Jesus was truly the Messiah, the rightful leader of God's people. It was a day of declaring allegiance to him by throwing in one's lot with the original apostolic band.

To be as explicit as possible let me perhaps overstate the point. It was not a matter of "receiving Jesus into their hearts," then finding a church of their choice for fellowship. It was not a matter of the inner experience of justification or even conversion first making them members of the spiritual or invisible body of Christ, later to be baptized and join the visible church. It was not a matter of "saving their souls," then joining voluntary religious societies called "believers churches." The ground of their justification was their act of repentance (*metanoia*), which in this case meant changing their minds about Jesus, and *baptism* which was a public declaration of their commitment to the new community.

Within the new group defined by allegiance to Jesus Christ they received the Holy Spirit, for it was the victorious Messiah and Lord of the new community who was giving the Spirit (Hull, 1967:71-72). The Spirit of the ascended Christ now became the Spirit of his new body. Peter's promise that following repentance and baptism they would receive the gift of the Holy Spirit (v. 38) was not the promise of a "second experience." It was the announcement that within the community of the Spirit the new reality is found.

Later this connection between the Spirit and the community is shown by the gift of the Spirit which comes when the apostles lay hands on new Christians (8:7; 19:6). This Spirit is the Spirit of the apostolic community. The Spirit is *not* the possession of the apostles, as we learn in the Cornelius story (10:44-48), but the hallmark and dynamic of the community.

Here, then, in the *koinonia* of the Spirit, is the key to the gospel as an announcement of present reality. The good news is of a community rooted in the Holy Spirit which is the instrument of our salvation. It is characterized by the "fruit of the Spirit"—the "more excellent way" of love. It is not created by sacramental consecration, theological announcement, ecstatic experience, or moralistic achievement. If such a reality of the Spirit does not exist, the gospel has little meaning in our contemporary secular existence.[16]

2

The Individual-in-Community in the Bible

In American society today, the unquestioned assumption is that the individual takes precedence over the group. Freedom means individual independence. Civil rights means the individual's right to "life, liberty, and the pursuit of happiness."

That the individual soul has infinite worth is a truism. All individuals must be allowed to make their own free moral decisions apart from social coercion. Salvation and religious convictions are preeminently personal—that is, private individual matters before God. The very word "sacred" indicates for us a degree of intimacy related to the secret recesses of the individual self and therefore a profoundly private experience.[1]

By the same token, the community is seen as a contractual association of free individuals. *Social* is the antonym of *personal*. The concept of a *corporate person* is a purely legal construct. The corporation and the social club (association) have become the conceptual models for community, even religious community. Indeed, the only recognized status of the church under the United States Constitution is that of a nonprofit corporation.

The concept of organic community has been heavily eroded by technology, urbanization, political ideology, and legal definitions. Even marriage and family are increasingly accepted as matters of individual contract and convenience. The group has become for us a collection of individuals created *by* individuals *for* their own individual advantages.

In contrast, the biblical culture emphasized the community as basic for human identity. Salvation is the work of God in creating covenant community. Jesus not only called individual disciples out from the "old" Israel, he began the formation of the "new Israel"—the messianic community. The Holy Spirit's work in the New Testament is the creation of the new community, and individuals receive the Spirit as they join in that *koinonia* of the Spirit through repentance and baptism (Acts 2:38). Christ committed the continuation of his mission to "his body, the church," and not simply to individual members of it (Matt. 16:18-19; 28:19-20).

But does not such emphasis on the priority of community threaten the unique value of the individual? How does one become a disciple of Jesus? What does it mean to be an individual Christian? What does it mean to attain mature personhood in the body of Christ (Eph. 4:12-13)? What is the place of the individual in the community witness? Does not such a social emphasis fly in the face of the great evangelical tradition of personal soul winning?

The impact of modern rational individualism has been overpowering in both liberal and fundamentalist Protestantism. As the public assumption or mind-set in America, it has influenced biblical interpretation for the last 150 years. In light of this we need to examine in detail the broader biblical assumptions and perspectives underlying the New Testament concept of the church as the messianic community. In this chapter, then, we shall look at biblical definitions which will give depth perspective to our understanding of the community of the Spirit.

The Biblical Context

The Bible, especially the New Testament, affirms the significance and worth of the individual. However, not all the implications we have come to accept as "gospel truth" stem from the Bible alone. We read our Bibles in the context of twentieth-century definitions and assumptions, and we tend to read our contemporary ideas into the Bible.

If read in the context of its own historical and cultural milieu, the Bible challenges some of our assumptions. Modern concepts of individualistic religion actually emerged during a long postbiblical historical development, and they originate from a variety of sources.[2]

The problem of alienation between the individual and society, so characteristic of the modern Western world, is foreign to the Bible. The cultural background against which it should be interpreted more closely resembles some contemporary African tribal cultures than American individualism. In these societies the individual is viewed as a particular embodiment of the organic family, literally tied to the ancestors as the continuation of their life force. The individual gains self-identity by assimilating the identity of the clan. John Taylor explains this in his book, *The Primal Vision*, in which he gives us a profound glimpse into African views of humanity and religion.

Man is literally a family tree, a single branching organism whose existence is continuous through time, and whose roots, though out of sight below the earth, may spread further and wider than all the visible limbs above. Death, it is true, makes a difference. . . . Yet in this single, continuing entity there is no radical distinction of being between that part of the family which is 'here' and that which is 'there.' A son's life is the prolongation of his father's life, of his grandfather's and of the whole lineage. . . .

The fact of individuality may often clash with the demands of this collective humanity, just as conflict often arises between father and son, and the occasions for this are far more numerous in these days. Yet the underlying conviction remains that an individual who is cut off from the communal organism is a nothing. . . . As the glow of a coal depends upon its remaining in the fire, so the vitality, the psychic security, the very humanity of a man, depends on his integration into the family (1963:99f.).

Viewed against this background, the biblical concept that individuals' relation to God determines their human identity can be seen as a liberating revelation. The conviction that individuals are responsible to God in a relation that transcends ties to family and tribe is the very ground of freedom. "For freedom Christ has set us free," wrote Paul to the Galatian Christians (5:1). And he continued by warning them not to submit again to bondage under the old tribal regulations and myths that had defined their self-identity (cf. Col. 2:9). Let us look more closely at the biblical data.

Individuality in the Old Testament

Just as the presuppositions of humanistic individualism provide the working definitions and assumptions of modern Western society, so the idea of group solidarity lay behind ancient Hebrew thought about humankind. We moderns assume that the individual person is prior to the collective group, and that community is formed by a contractual arrangement of free individuals for their own mutual purposes.

The ancients assumed that the community was the source and security of the individual. The group and the individual existed in solidarity. Humankind, as they understood it, is like a great tree with its roots, trunk, limbs, and leaves. Living individuals are like the leaves of the tree. They are ephemeral, dependent units in the collective life of the ongoing social group. In such a view, based on an analogy with nature, individuals' identity and significance were totally determined by the group. They had no personal independence or value in themselves.

Seen against the backdrop of this ancient tribal view, the Old Testament concept of the individual-in-community under the covenant of Yahweh emerges in its true perspective and significance. It clearly breaks with the nature analogy and presents a unique understanding of the individual in relation to God who transcends the community. This basic divergence with tribal concepts found growing expression in the life of Israel, as prophetic interpreters explored the implications of their faith in Yahweh.

A thorough historical review of the Old Testament and Jewish concepts of human identity is beyond the scope of this chapter; however, a summary of significant concepts which provide the background and basis for the Christian approach is important.[3] We must constantly remind ourselves of the importance of distinctive Old Testament ideas for our interpretation of the New. This is especially important in light of the powerful influence of modern Western individualism on our biblical interpretations.

First, then, we must note that the primal human reality recognized in the Old Testament is the community —the corporate, social reality. As G. Ernest Wright has observed, the formation of community is God's central act according to the Old Testament. He writes,

> What to us and to most of the world's religions should be the dominant concern—namely, the life of the individual in his world—is in the Bible relegated to an important but nevertheless secondary position. God has brought into being, through redemptive acts which have culminated in Christ, a community in which each individual is called to participate. Individual and community are held together in a viable relationship without either being lost in concentration upon the other. Yet the formation of the community is God's central act . . . (1954:18f.).

God made his covenant with the community of Israel as a whole people. Indeed, Israel both in time and space was considered one community before God, and the covenant of salvation was the source of Israel's identity. The covenant was first established with Israel's forefather, Abraham, in whose "loins" it was believed the community already existed. Then it was renewed at Sinai, through Moses, with the whole people who had come out of Egypt. Individuals were brought under the covenant of promise by being incorporated into the "commonwealth of Israel" through birth or conversion.

The community, or people, of Israel were viewed as a single personal reality or "corporate personality."[4] On the one hand, the "people" or tribe was identified with its ancestor. For example, "Israel" may refer to the whole people or to the ancestral father, Jacob. On the other hand, individual Israelites had their personal identity as "sons and daughters of Israel."

Social identity was primary, and individuals found their self-identity through incorporation and participation in this social reality. Thus they participated in the covenant as members of the corporate person, Israel. "Throughout the whole period of the Old Testament," wrote H. Wheeler Robinson, "this covenant with the 'corporate personality' of Israel (as we may call it) remains the all-inclusive fact and factor, whatever the increase in the consciousness of individuality" (1964:26-27).

In Old Testament society the worst fate individuals could suffer was to be cut off from their inheritance among God's people.[5] By contrast, the greatest blessing was to be completely joined to and identified with God's people in a festival of worship. Individualism could only be viewed as alienation. Personal fulfillment came through allying oneself with the life and purposes of the group.

Creation Stories
This view of the individual human being as a social person is evident in the creation stories. According to these accounts the individual was made for communi-

ty. This is indicated in a variety of ways: 1) in the use of the word *adam* for both the individual and collective humankind; 2) in the concept of the "image of God" as relational (social); and 3) in the content of the covenant. Let us examine each of these ideas.

First, *adam*, which is predominantly a generic term for humankind, is used in both creation accounts to designate the highest creature God made. It designates both *a man* and *humankind* (including male and female), in such a way that even when one person seems most obviously intended, what is said applies equally to all humankind. *Adam*, the first human couple, is both the representative and precursor of the race, in whom the race already exists.

Thus it is the *human family* that stands at the pinnacle of the creation process, and not the perfected, rational, individual male of Aristotelian vintage.[6] In the biblical perspective, the human family (community) living under God's covenant of peace (*shalom*) is the goal of creation. If this at first appears to be a negative point, that is only because rationalistic individualism has made the individual the epitome of human evolution and value.

Second, according to the Genesis accounts, human beings in the totality of their physical-social being were made "in the image of God." The image is not a special rational-spiritual faculty inserted or breathed into them, but a godlike characteristic of humans in the totality of their being. It is an essential character associated with *adam* as a *social creature*. It is not a spiritual nature added to the physical and social faculties. It is not an image of God *in* humankind. It is described as the endowment of the total creature with a spiritual quality, perception, or capacity which makes possible a unique relationship with God.

Further, it is not a rational or spiritual nature which makes it possible for individuals to have a mystical knowledge of God apart from their historical and social existence. Rather, it is a capacity which makes it possible for them to realize the transcendent dimensions of personal being through responsible, loving relationships both to God and to fellow humans. Human beings express the image through their participation as persons in the human community. In more traditional theological terminology, *Adam as representative of humankind* is in the image of God, and each person bears the image through participation in *adam*.

If this concept remains an abstraction for us, it is because we have not experienced the profound reality of personal solidarity and interdependence in community. Perhaps we can better understand what is being said if we rephrase it. Individual human beings in their aloneness and alienation are not the bearers of the image of God, but reconciled men and women in relationship to God and their fellows. Until the individual is in responsible relationship, we can only speak of the image as a capacity or potential.

Further, we note that the image of God is immediately associated with humankind's ability to hear and respond to God's covenant. *Adam* is the *covenant creature*—the creature who in his and her very essence is socially responsible. All human beings stand responsible under God's covenant for fellow human beings and for the earth on which they have been placed.

By covenant definition, humans are in social and spiritual solidarity with every other human being, and they realize the unique dimensions of the divine image in their response to the covenant which the Creator made with them. Hence to fully understand the essential nature of God's image we must observe the terms of the covenant the Creator made with them.

Third, as we have just noted, the covenant which defined the human family's responsibility and, by inference, its nature deals with life in society and the natural order. The covenant gives the human family both a social and ecological mandate. Not only in the Genesis accounts, but also in the writings of the prophets, the point is explicitly made that the covenant is not concerned in the first place with special religious duties. It is not focused on sacrificial offerings and liturgy which humanity owes to God.

The command to *Adam* was not to make sacrifices but to "subdue" (bring order) and have dominion under God over the earth (Gen. 1:26, 28). That is what we today call the *ecological* mandate. Further, humankind was to multiply and fill the earth with their own kind. That is the *social-cultural* mandate. And these mandates were to be kept as a profound spiritual responsibility to God, the Creator. That is the *religious* dimension, which should pervade all of life.

According to the covenant, the goal of creation was a community of *shalom*. In nonreligious language, it was a responsible, mutually supportive human society living in harmony with and as part of the ecosystem under the covenant of God.

The primal reality is the human community in which

the individual as a participating member finds self-awareness and personhood. In the Old Testament, personhood is not predicated on a humanistic base, either social or individual. It does not visualize human society as a collective of independent rational individual persons who have autonomous individual identity, status, and rights apart from or prior to responsible social interaction. *Adam*, the human creature, is, as *person*, an *individual-in-community*.

The definition of humanity's unique personhood is grounded on the biblical understanding of God as personal, and on the covenant as an absolute moral (not natural) law addressed both to the individual and the community. In those ancient cultures that worshiped nature gods, the individual tended to be submerged in nature and the clan. Not so in Israel. Although there was a profound awareness of the solidarity of the individuals in community, nevertheless each individual was believed to have a unique responsibility to God, and thus a unique status in the community.

We might note here parenthetically that this is in sharp contrast to the contemporary New Age movements. They, like the ancient religions, ground human solidarity and individuality in nature. In New Age thought the oneness of the human race is a metaphysical oneness, not the social unity of love. Thus according to New Age philosophy, individual uniqueness can be achieved only by self-assertion (We will return to this point at the end of the chapter.) Such a philosophy might serve as a basis for modern individualism, but it is a far cry from the biblical concept of human solidarity.

Consider how the following kinds of data infer the recognition of individual responsibility before God. The people of Israel were formed not on the basis of blood, but of covenant which implies individual response and submission. The "Ten Words," spoken by God in Exodus 20 are given in the singular—"Thou shalt. . . ." They are not only spoken to the collective as a collective, but to the individual within the group.

Transgression of the covenant was considered not only to be against the community but against God's own self. Collective retribution plays no part as a principle of punishment in the covenant as recorded in Exodus 20—23. Love for God and the neighbor is made the ground and motive for obedience to the covenant law, and love is a highly personal motivation. Such an appeal could only be made to an individual.[7]

G. Ernest Wright has observed that in the Deuteronomic restatement of the covenant law there is an "alternation between the plural and singular forms of address" that is quite bewildering unless "both community and individual were constantly in mind." He points out that the community law of Israel was by no means a "tribal ethic," and he continues with an excellent description of the relation of the individual to the community order

> Yet the individual was not lost or submerged in this community order. In it God's *"Thou shalt"* was characteristically singular, addressed to each individual. God's Word in the law singled out each person, so that as a responsible 'I' the individual heard the Word to the nation as being addressed to him [or her] personally. Man was not an insignificant and unsegregated component of a tribal mass.

There was no such thing as "mass society" in which the individual had no knowledge of himself, or of responsible selfhood, or of direct access to the sovereign power whose authority was absolute. In the covenant with the nation God dignified each member with his personal address, so that each one understood the responsible nature of his relationship to the Divine Person (1954:25f.).

We must make a distinction between *individuality* and *individualism* in discussing Old Testament concepts. The former calls attention to the individual as a responsible person in community, while the latter exalts the independence of individuals and their private rights. Individuality is affirmed in the form and content of the covenant; individualism is considered a matter of alienation and pride.

The sin of humankind is not the assertion of individuality in community, but the assertion of individual self-sufficiency and independence from God and fellow humans. This point is made in many ways. *Adam* grasped for knowledge that would give self-sufficiency and self-gratification. "You shall be as gods!" said the tempter. Cain refused to take responsibility for his brother (Gen. 4:9). In the days of Noah the earth was full of competitive violence (Gen. 6:5). The sin of the inhabitants of Babel was their collective self-assertion to make a name for themselves and to insure their immortality as a master race (Gen. 11:4). So the dreary story continued.

But in none of these accounts is sin identified as individual recognition of rights and responsibilities. Indeed, Noah and Abraham, the two patriarchs who represent new beginnings, are called as individuals to break with tribal identification and conformity. Contrary to some earlier interpretations of the Old Testament as presenting a typical tribal view of human identity, these stories show a profound understanding of individual self-awareness and responsibility before God. At the same time, they assume and idealize solidarity of the social group. They are sensitive to the sins which grow out of individualism—namely unfair competition between weak and strong and the alienation and inequalities that result from it.

The Prophets and Psalms

The peak of individual religious and moral responsibility in the Old Testament may be found in the writings of the prophets. Indeed, the spiritual self-consciousness of the prophet became the prototype for New Testament religious experience. A brief glance at the prophetic consciousness is, therefore, important.

First, the prophets were profoundly conscious of themselves as the servants of God under the covenant made with Israel. Their essential message to the people was that they should turn from their sin and serve God in covenant relation. But even as they spoke for God, they assumed their own solidarity with Israel. For example, when they confessed Israel's sin they included themselves—"We have sinned." As channels of the Word of God to Israel, they called Israel to peoplehood under the covenant, not merely to an individual religious experience.

This individual self-awareness as spokespersons for God provided them the ground and courage to challenge the king, the corporate head of the nation. Indeed, this was the kind of God-awareness that marked the authentic prophet. The self-identity of the court prophets merged with that of the nation. They identified God's voice with the will of the national leader and spoke what the king wanted to hear. The prophets of the Lord, on the other hand, distinguished between the voice of God and the national ego, and they spoke as individual representatives of God to the nation.

The writings of Jeremiah and Ezekiel reflect a new clarity of prophetic individual self-awareness. They prophesied at a time when the identity of the people as a nation was at its lowest point, yet their solidarity with the community of Israel and their vision of the renewal of the covenant community are clear. The new spiritual awareness of individual responsibility before God did not lead toward individualism. It bred a new understanding of the nature of authentic community in which the bond is neither blood nor law but the Spirit of God.

In his Lamentations over the fall of Judah as a nation, Jeremiah alternates between the use of the third person (they) and the first person (we), and between singular and plural (I, we). The effect is to make his individual self-consciousness and his self-identity as one member of Judah simultaneously transparent. Even though rejected and persecuted by his own people, he views his own fate and that of the nation as inextricably interwoven. The nation's fate is his fate. Yet out of his own sense of individual calling and inner certainty of God's Word to him (Jer. 1:5-10), this same Jeremiah prophesied most clearly the character of the new covenant law. This law would be written on the hearts of individuals so each person would know the Lord personally (31:31-34).

In similar fashion Ezekiel, who speaks so forthrightly about the individuality of guilt and punishment (18:1-10), records his vision of the future resurrection of the *nation* by the Spirit of God (37:11-14). He speaks of the restoration of the temple—a corporate symbol of religious experience and allegiance. Individual identity and corporate solidarity are equally part of his experience. The individual and the community are complementarities in his view of humankind.

The other major record of individuality in the Old Testament is in the Psalms. Undoubtedly, we should not read modern individualistic experience into the language of the Psalms. Yet who can read the prayers of confession with their depths of introspection, or the expressions of lonely trust and confidence in God, and fail to be impressed with the degree of individual self-awareness before God (see, for example, Ps. 32:3-5; 62:1-2)?

However, in virtually the same breath the Psalmist expresses the solemn joy of solidarity with God's people in the act of worship, and the anguish of being cut off from Israel. The very meaning of individuals' lives is represented as bound up with their participation in the corporate body of Israel.

In summary, even a sketchy overview of the Old Testament concept of the relation of individuals and communities testifies to the wide divergence between the prophetic ideal and rational individualism. It offers us a distinctly different basis for community than we have in the Lockean idea that underlies our American political community. John Locke viewed community as an association of individuals formed exclusively for the mutual enhancement and protection of individual rights. This latter model, which has dominated our own sense of both religious and political community, is quite foreign to the prophets!

Individuality Under the New Covenant

A striking aspect of Jesus' ministry was his concern for the individual person.[8] To him, the individual was not simply a specimen belonging to a class. He did not classify persons as Samaritans, publicans, Pharisees, fishermen, or Zealots. His choice of disciples exemplifies this. They were a widely divergent group—covering the whole spectrum from Galilee to Judea, aristocrats to fisher folk and farmers, collaborating tax collectors to defiant Zealots. In personal exchanges Jesus recognized each individual's unique self-identity and aspirations. He related to persons according to their own inner longings and resolve. He did not depersonalize individuals by viewing them as types.

Jesus' self-identity was grounded in his awareness of a special relationship to God as his Father. This should not come as a surprise. The story of man's and woman's creation directly implies that they came to know who they were only as they were individually confronted by God. Jesus clearly had a distinctive self-awareness of a relationship to God unmediated by priest or Torah. He had a sense of destiny quite exclusively his own, but that destiny bound him to his community in an original vicarious design of dependence and transcendence.

Like every human individual, Jesus achieved his sense of psychological and social personhood through interaction in a historical community. The listing of his genealogy locates him in that historical tradition and clearly implies this (Matt. 1:1-16; Luke 3:23-38.) Paul also recognizes Jesus' cultural conditioning when he describes him in Gal. 4:4 as "born of woman, *born under the law*" (emphasis added).

Jesus' Jewish community was the conditioning matrix in which he experienced his spiritual self-identity, but this self-awareness as the Christ was given to him in a relationship to God that transcended the community.[9] The Gospel writers represent the source as a voice from heaven at his baptism and the gift of the Holy Spirit which he received "without measure" (John 3:34-35).

Jesus' way of seeing others was related to his own self-identity as a unique Son of God.[10] His was not the self-awareness of a "Fuehrer" who relates as one unique individual to the masses. Indeed, he spoke of himself as a "Servant," as (in psychological terms) one who recognized others' full freedom as children of God. His own self-perception made him sensitive to the identity of each person, and his ministry offered to many the first recognition and acceptance of themselves as persons.

The new dimensions of personal realization which are disclosed in the life of Jesus become the model for all who will acknowledge him as Lord. Just as Jesus' own unique personal identity was confirmed by the Holy Spirit when he heard the words, "beloved Son," so Paul says we have been given the Holy Spirit to bring us to full recognition that we are beloved children (Rom. 8:14-16).[11] Our most profound self-awareness is attained in confrontation with Ultimate Reality—and in the Christian experience of individuality that ultimate reality is known as the Holy Spirit.

Speaking psychologically, this is the significance of Jesus' special gift of the Holy Spirit to his disciples as he left the historical scene. It was expedient for them, he said, that he go away so that the Spirit could come (John 16:7). Their own maturity as individuals could not be attained in a continuing attachment to him as earthly teacher. Only in a new transcending awareness of God the Spirit could they receive new self-awareness—a new identity and confidence. The Spirit would be their guide to truth. The Spirit would make possible new intimacy of relation with God, would give authentic selfhood.

This new dimension of awareness and identity was anticipated by the prophets, and specifically foretold by Jeremiah and Joel. Jeremiah spoke of the new inward perception of God's covenant law (Jer. 31:33-34). Joel predicted the time when God's Spirit would be poured out on individuals of every age, sex, and class among God's people (2:28-29). Luke understood this prophecy of Joel to have been fulfilled at Pentecost. This was when the prophetic self-consciousness became the common denominator of all those in the new messianic community (Acts 2:17-18). God's Spirit had created a new personal identity in the new community of the Spirit.

In the Pauline epistles, the phrases "in Christ" and "Christ in you" denote this new dimension of personal identity. No longer is self-concept formed through identification with Israel "after the flesh," that is, the old social reality. The new pattern is achieved through identification with Jesus Christ, who represents the new Israel, the true children of Abraham.

The new self-image of "Christ in you" supersedes all the old categories that depersonalized and collectivized men and women. "In Christ" the old categories of discrimination and prejudice are abolished (Gal. 2:25-28; Col. 3:10-11). Every individual has been given new dignity and status as a "child of God" and a "member of God's household." The new community is a community of new individuals.

Personhood in Community

We have said that Jesus gave new importance and dignity to the individual, but we should not conclude that he was disinterested in social transformation. Jesus came to establish authentic community, and to this end he called individuals to new spiritual awareness under the rule of God. His was not a ministry of releasing individuals from the web of physical and social relationships through inner spiritual enlightenment. (That was the goal of Lord Buddha, not Lord Jesus!) He called individuals to new dimensions of self-awareness and personhood in *the new* covenant community.

Jesus' self-awareness as the Messiah and Son of God involved him in intimate identification with and participation in his social community. That is what *incarnation* means! And the purpose of his incarnation, of his complete identification with us, was to inaugurate the *new age of the Spirit* in which the new individual-in-covenant community would be formed according to God's original intention. The new identity of Jesus' followers as children of God and participants in the messianic mission involved them in a koinonia under the new covenant which he initiated. Awareness of new individual identity before God inevitably and necessarily *involves one in community*. Life in the Spirit is a life of new openness to others in a fellowship of reconciliation.

The new consciousness and appreciation of the individual's place in the community is indicated by the appeal of New Testament writers to Abraham as "father of the faithful." The model for the new covenant is the Abrahamic covenant and not the Mosaic. Both Paul and Jesus himself appealed to Abraham and the Abrahamic covenant as the prototype for the new covenant community.

Of course the Abrahamic and Mosaic covenants are not conflicting or even divergent in intent, but they do differ in historical circumstance and therefore in construction and character. The covenant with Abraham was made with an individual. In form it was a personal agreement without an elaborate code. It required loyalty and good faith and thus provided a basis for a new relationship. Abraham's new self-identity as the "ancestor of many nations" (TEV) was based simply on God's covenant promise (Gen. 17:5ff.).

In the Mosaic covenant, the contracting parties are God and the "mixed multitude" that had come out of Egypt. In form the Mosaic covenant was a legal agreement requiring faithful obedience to Torah (Law) on

Israel's part. Its purpose was the formation of a people, of a national religious community. Thus while the Mosaic covenant was in historical continuity with the Abrahamic, it did not represent its fulfillment. A national community under a legal covenant (Torah) was not, and is not, the ultimate intention of the promise to Abraham.[12]

The messianic covenant established a community of personal relationship and loyalty based on repentance and commitment. This community was no longer based on a legal-cultural agreement rooted in the biological family and its religious tradition. (Note how Abraham was called to break with his family and its religious tradition.)

In both kinds of community the individual finds personal identity in community, but with a difference. Under the Mosaic covenant, individual identity was found "in Israel," that is, in identification with the religious-cultural tradition of the ancestors. It was not merely coincidence that Jewish boys were declared "sons of the Law" as they were initiated into adult status in the community. Under the new covenant, self-identity is found "in Christ." The Spirit of Christ gives form and dynamic to the new community in which individuals find their self-actualization and identity.

Through the disclosure of the risen Christ as the living Spirit, a new perception of the interrelation of individual and community became possible. Christ as the Spirit became the formative principle (Word) and creative reality (Life) of the new koinonia. Christ is the light which enlightens everyone coming into it.

Or in a different figure, Christ pours out the Spirit

on each individual in the community (Acts 2:4, 17). He is called "head of the body," and the community is said to subsist in him (Col. 2:19). Thus the individuals are related to the community by a relationship to Christ. They achieve their self-actualization in the community through a relationship to him that transcends the community.[13]

This transcendent relationship gives the individual a new standing in relation to the community. The new self-realization is not without the community. There is no more possibility of personal identity in Christ apart from the brother and sister than there is of loving Christ without loving them (1 John 4:20). But both psychologically and spiritually a new freedom, and a new quality of participation and interdependence, has been achieved in Christ. A new criterion of worth is established. A new definition of the person as "spiritual" becomes possible. And all this is possible only through *koinonia—community in Christ*!

The "New Age" Model of Individual Self-Realization

We have seen that the biblical model of personhood assumes and teaches that individuals achieve their full self-realization only in covenant relation to God and other human beings. The actualization of the *image of God* in human beings is fully realized only as they find their self-identity as *persons-in-covenant community*. In biblical terms such self-fulfillment is known as "salvation." And salvation involves not only isolated individuals in relation to God, but also the creation of community under God.

In this age of individualism there are many religious and philosophical ideologies that dispute this model of self-fulfillment. Some of these claim to be Christian. Others, such as the "New Age" philosophies, explicitly claim to revive pre-Christian pagan ideas.

"Christian" schemes deal almost exclusively with individual salvation. They define the salvation experience in terms of a private, inward, even mystical experience with God. They often use the language of pop psychology and stress self-potential, feeling good about one's self, achieving one's goals, and maximizing *real* pleasure. Then they link all this to a "born again" experience with Jesus. For such people an "electronic church" which preaches a gospel of success is sufficient to satisfy their egos. The individualism of this kind of Christianity has much in common with the "New Age" aspirations, although it differs greatly in its philosophical assumptions.

The New Age philosophies speak of transformation, unity with nature and the Cosmic Mind. In their scheme, self-actualization comes by transcending the limitations of bodily perception in an experience of "cosmic consciousness." New Age devotees decry the rationalistic individualism of our society; they teach a way of self-realization through mystical connection with the cosmos as a whole.

The key concept here is "unity with," not "community." According to their thought, one does not find individual identity and fulfillment through personal confrontation with God and social interaction within a community of salvation. Rather, people find fulfillment through an inward, mystical journey in which self-identity comes by way of metaphysical identification with "the All." By contrast, the biblical concept articulates an outward movement of forgiveness and reconciliation, of personal interdependence and sharing of God's purpose for the cosmos.

Such a concept of the self as an essential aspect of the All, or, as some teach, "god," results in strange paradoxes in the different New Age systems. On the one hand, it suggests that "the identities associated with all levels of consciousness are illusory, except for the ultimate level of Mind," and "all individuality dissolves into universal, undifferentiated oneness."[14] On the other hand the idea that each individual is in essence god—though not all of god—is used as the basis for individual worth and the right to actualize one's distinct self-identity.

If the individual is divine, the proper end of life is self-actualization, or the realization of ones "unlimited potential," as New Agers teach. Thus the individual's focus is turned inward on self rather than outward in concern and responsibility for others. Self-actualization becomes a matter of self-discovery and self-assertion. The result is individual autonomy, not community. Thus a movement which begins in reaction to modern individualism refocuses on the individual self at the expense of community.

Jesus also spoke of the paradoxical experience of losing self to find self, and of denying self to fulfill one's true self. In his terms, "to lose oneself" means to renounce the rights of divinity and to submit oneself in service to the neighbor. Under the rule of God we do not make self, but God the center. Only then do we find true "self-actualization," in harmony with the full selfhood of others through authentic community.

The "kingdom of God" which Jesus promoted is a community, or koinonia, of individuals in submission to the authority of God's covenant of "life and peace" (Mal. 2:5). Such a community affirms individuality and makes *agape* the bond of unity. Instead of an inward search for metaphysical unity with the universe, the movement is outward to others in forgiveness and reconciliation. Instead of self-assertion and independence, individuals seek the fulfillment of their personal potential in interdependence and the sharing of concern for each other.

3

Jesus and
the Community

The history of the new community which we call
church begins with the life and ministry of Jesus. Each
of the four Gospels indicates this in its own way. But
this is not an absolute beginning without antecedents,
as the Gospels also recognize and indicate.

Specifically, Matthew and Luke relate what began
with Jesus to the past by presenting us with genealo-
gies. Matthew traces the beginning to Abraham (1:1-
17), and Luke traces it back to "Adam, the son of God"
(3:38). John begins his account with a prologue that introduces Jesus as the embodiment of the "Word" of
God which was already expressed in creation and has
been in the world ever since (1:1-14). Mark is less explicit. He, however, links the "gospel" to the message
of the prophets and to John the Baptist who represents
that tradition. But more of this later.

The appearance of Jesus as the Christ represents a
new beginning in God's relation to the human race,
but it is a beginning within the chain of history. We
used the figure of gestation and birth to describe the
emergence of the church on the day of Pentecost. According to Luke that gestation period can be traced
back to the first human being. Already at "the beginning" the Spirit and the Word were active creating hu-

man community, and the church is understood as the flowering of that activity.

It is important to link the community that formed on the day of Pentecost with this universal activity of God. This linkage indicates that the church was not created to be an exclusive religious community to exist alongside the various other religious communities. God's intention for the church is universal blessing. The same Spirit that hovered over the chaos in creation creating light and order in the universe was also active in the conception of Jesus, then in the formation of the new community of Jesus. In each case the Spirit's activity had a universal purpose.

Matthew traces Jesus' ancestry beyond David and the Israelite kingdom back to Abraham through whom it was promised that "all the nations of the earth shall be blessed" (Gen. 18:18). Unfortunately, in Jesus' day Israel had become an exclusive community which understood its universal destiny as the imperialistic domination of the nations. Matthew is convinced that a new kind of community is necessary. It must be one through which the promise of blessing to all nations can be fulfilled without domination of one nation over others. Jesus and his church are that new beginning.

The Church in the Gospels

For many years the relation of Jesus to the organization we call "church" has been debated. Harnack, a liberal theologian and historian at the beginning of this century, argued that Jesus had no intention of founding a new community. His message was the kingdom of God, which was to rule human hearts. Harnack thought Jesus was primarily concerned with the moral and spiritual renewal of individuals who would spread the kingdom of God through their relationships in society at large. This set off a half century of debate over whether Jesus intended to found the church.

The debate has gone through several twists and turns we cannot follow here in detail. Scholars like Bultmann, who denied the very possibility of knowing what the "historical Jesus" was like, concluded that we could not know Jesus' intention. At the same time he and other "form critics" were pointing out how profoundly the Gospel accounts were conditioned by the life and situation of the first churches. This insight into the integral relation between the narrative of the Gospels and the life of the early church opened a new approach to the question.

Whether or not it is possible to resolve the question of Jesus' private intentions, we can know how the apostles and first church leaders understood Jesus' relation to events that followed. Their obvious assumption is that the "*ekklēsiai*," or churches, are the authentic continuation of the ministry of Jesus. They understood his resurrection as God's vindication of his messiahship. And they saw themselves as having been commissioned by him to continue what he had begun.

Perhaps this debate has grown partly out of ambiguity in terms. If by church we mean the religious institution that developed from the second century on, it is doubtful the earthly Jesus would have envisioned it. Certainly nothing in the accounts suggests he did. But if by church we mean the initial network of disciple communities who made up the movement of faith and witness, then it is clear Jesus' immediate disciples thought he had intended such a development.

Beginning with this presupposition, scholars like R. Newton Flew, writing fifty years ago, and Gerhard Lohfink, New Testament professor at Tubingen University today, have carefully examined the Gospels to determine what Jesus must have had in mind.[1]

Mark

The Gospel of Mark is least explicit in its reference to an ongoing movement. Mark's opening statement about the "beginning of the gospel" should be set in the context of the post-resurrection Christian community. That is the setting in which Mark was written. This certainly implies that the gospel which was the gospel the churches were preaching. The gospel was and is the story of Jesus as it began with John the Baptist (cf. Acts 1:22).

The word "gospel" in passages like Mark 1:1, 13:10, and 14:9 refers to more than the preaching of the earthly Jesus.[2] It is at the same time the "gospel of the kingdom" which Jesus preached *and* the gospel about Jesus as the Christ crucified, risen, and glorified in the church which the apostles were preaching. The longer ending of Mark mentions that the resurrected Jesus commanded the disciples to proclaim this gospel in the whole world. It closes with the report that in obedience to Jesus they "proclaimed the good news everywhere" (16:15, 20, NRSV).

Such a coming together of meanings in Mark's use of the word gospel implies the "continuity of the theological message" as well as "continuity of historical event"

(Hengel, 1985:53f.). Certainly Mark assumes that Jesus is the self-conscious, historical source of the continuing movement. But beyond that we can say little.

Matthew

The Gospel of Matthew is far more explicit in its references to Jesus and the church. It is the only Gospel in which the word *ekklēsia* appears (16:18; 18:17). Clearly Matthew understood Jesus to have intentionally set the stage for the continuing movement that followed the resurrection. He views Jesus' ministry as the origin and basis of the new people of God. His teaching provided the new covenant law fulfilling and superseding the old (chapters 5—7). His death—the shedding of his blood—is the covenant sacrifice which establishes the new community (26:28).

According to Matthew's understanding, the church is the true Israel, which has displaced the national Jewish state that officially rejected Jesus as the Messiah. The Jewish leaders were likened to the tenant farmers of a vineyard who rejected the landlord's ownership and finally killed his son who came to collect rent (21:33ff.). The true Israelites are those who recognize Jesus as the Messiah and become his disciples. These are the ones who hear and do what he commands, thus recognizing his authority. Here there is clear continuity between the old and the new people of God. True Israelites under both covenants are the children of Abraham, the ancestor of the Christ (3:9; 8:11).

For Matthew the concept of discipleship is central. As Jack Kingsbury says, it is "by analyzing Matthew's portrait of the disciples that one gains insight into his understanding of the church" (1986:82).[3] By definition a disciple is one who learns from the master by observation and imitation. "Following" implies both activities. It is not enough to hear the teaching. Doing what the master says is of the essence (7:21-29). The church is the community of the disciples of Jesus, that is, those who own Jesus' authority and are learning to pattern their lives after his. And the commission of the church is to "make disciples of all nations" (28:19-20).

Further, the church of Matthew is that community which recognizes that the rule of God is present in the authority of Jesus as Messiah. It was when Peter said of Jesus, "You are the Messiah, the Son of the living God," that Jesus responded, "on this rock I will build my church" (16:16-18, NRSV). Jesus did not promise to build his church on Peter the superior apostle, but on Peter the confessor of his messianic authority. Indeed, almost immediately Peter demonstrated how fallible and weak he would be as an individual. He did not even understand the meaning of his own confession.[4]

Jesus gave the "keys of the kingdom of heaven" (16:19; 18:18) to this community of disciples who recognized his authority to inaugurate the rule of God "on earth as it is in heaven."[5] These are the same keys he himself used as the messianic representative of faithful Israel. Israel had been called to be God's servant and make known God's gracious authority on earth. But like Jonah, who was called to warn Nineveh and offer it salvation in the name of Yahweh, they refused to carry out the mission (12:39; 16:4). Now Jesus was forming a new covenant people to carry out this responsibility, and he said the keys would be taken from the unfaithful Israel who rejected his authority (21:43).[6]

These keys represent the authority of Christ entrusted to the church. The disciple community has been authorized to make binding decisions in the name and spirit of Christ. But this authority is not delegated to the church as a new religious institution. The church's authority does not reside in its status as a superior religious institution superseding Israel. It has authority only because Jesus continues to be with it. That authority resides in the church's *dependence on Christ* and its *authenticity as a disciple community*. Therefore there must be discernment and agreement that its decisions represent the true spirit and will of Jesus (18:18-20).

In a special way the keys represent Jesus' authorization of the messianic community to free people from their bondage. This authentic community has the capacity to open doors firmly locked by ignorance, alienation, and fear. The community is authorized to forgive and thus free people from their shame, fear, and guilt. The keys are thus for the purpose of opening doors to reconciliation and healing. As William Klassen has reminded us, the church is the "community of forgiveness," a "fellowship of reconciliation."

Such forgiveness is "in the name of Jesus." This means it is a freeing which comes from accepting the way of Christ—the way of *agape* and the cross. The keys are to a life of "love, joy, and peace" in the kingdom of God, and Jesus is Lord of that kingdom.

Forgiveness follows repentance. To repent means to submit oneself to the discipline of Christ; to reorient oneself to the rule of God. Thus one enters the kingdom of God. And if not, the keys do not open the doors to healing and life. Such freedom is not achieved by asserting one's independence and rights.

To summarize, the church in Matthew is the disciple community commissioned by Jesus to continue his authoritative ministry. It is to introduce people to the reality of God's rule and call them to live in "righteousness and peace and joy" (Rom. 14:17) under the freedom of God's gracious authority.

Luke

Luke has his own perspectives and approaches to the relation of Jesus and the church. He sees the relation as one of historical development (Acts 1:1-2). What began with the announcements to Zechariah and Mary (Luke 1:11, 26) continues after the resurrection with the announcement of the two angels to the disciples (Acts 1:10-11). The mission of the earthly Jesus and the church is one continuous action of God's Spirit.[7]

Luke opens his gospel with a burst of Holy Spirit activity. The Spirit overshadows and empowers Mary to be the mother of the Messiah (1:35). The Spirit inspires Zechariah to prophesy the coming of the new era (1:67). The Spirit reveals to Simeon that the baby Jesus was indeed the promised Messiah (2:25). Then the Spirit comes upon Jesus in a special manifestation at his baptism (3:22) and thereafter Jesus is "full of the Holy Spirit" and moves at the prompting of the Spirit (4:1).

Following his period of temptation Jesus returns to the field of his ministry "filled with the power of the

Spirit" (4:14, NRSV), and this power is demonstrated in his ability to heal and forgive sins (5:17, 20). Thereafter Luke makes little direct reference to the Holy Spirit, but it is clear he understands Jesus' ministry as the direct manifestation of the power of God's Spirit (12:10).

The book of Acts begins with a parallel burst of Spirit activity, as we shall see in more detail. The Gospel of Luke does not end with a commissioning of the disciples, such as we have in Matthew. Rather they are told to "wait in Jerusalem" for the promise of the Spirit (24:49). Acts begins with Jesus' promise that the Holy Spirit will empower them for the task of witnessing (1:8). After a period of "waiting" (the gestation paralleled to Mary's wait), the new movement is born of the Spirit on Pentecost. And so the story continues with the Spirit firmly in charge, directing and empowering the mission.

In Acts, Luke describes the church as a movement which operates "in the name of Jesus" and comes to be called "Christian." Thus he indicates that the church takes its precedents from Jesus himself. Researcher Luke tells the story of Jesus' ministry in his own way (Luke 1:1-4). We can understand Luke's unique emphases by examining the way he differs from Matthew and Mark in telling the story. Luke's choice of teachings and events, and his editing of the materials, help us discover his view of the church and its mission. Several distinctive features stand out.

As Luke tells the story Jesus seems to have had a wider audience in mind than Mark and Matthew might indicate. Only Luke tells about Jesus' attempt to make contact in Samaria (9:51). And only he tells the parable of the "good Samaritan" (10:29-37). Jesus ministers to a Roman centurion, and to women like Joanna of Herod's court. He is quoted, "I came to cast fire upon the earth . . ." (12:49)—a saying that seems to indicate a universal mission.

The way in which Luke tells the story of Jesus sending out the disciples two by two also indicates Jesus had a broader vision of mission. Luke begins his special section with the story of three would-be disciples who were willing to follow Jesus on their own terms (9:1ff.). Then follows the account of Jesus sending seventy (or seventy-two) evangelist disciples "of another kind" (*heteros*) into the surrounding territory *where he intended to go* (10:1-16).

When Matthew refers to this event he leaves the impression that it was only the twelve disciples who were sent out (10:1, 5ff.). But Luke uses the symbolic number of seventy, which suggests a mission to all the nations.[8] And he suggests that they are simply extending Jesus' mission according to his own intention.

The sending "two by two" parallels the apparent practice in the apostolic church as its leaders crossed cultures with the message—take, for instance, Peter and John, Paul and Silas, Barnabas and John Mark. The commission (vv. 3-9) suggests an order of priority in the process of the mission.

First, they were to identify with the culture to which they had gone (depend on the local residents, and "eat what is set before you"). Second, they were to demonstrate the reality of God's saving authority ("heal the sick"). Last, they were to explain the significance of what was happening ("say . . . 'The kingdom of God has come near to you' "). This is an excellent approach for cross-cultural mission, and Luke presents it as a part of Jesus' own program.

Finally, Luke finds a precedent for the church's spiritual ministry of healing and forgiving in Jesus' own ministry. Whereas Matthew tends to view the act of forgiving as an authority delegated to the church, Luke views it as a ministry empowered by the Spirit. Forgiveness and healing are closely associated. As we have noted, Luke mentions that the power of the Spirit was given to Jesus to heal and to forgive (5:17, 20). That same power was given to the church "in the name of Jesus." When the resurrected Christ "opened their minds to understand the scriptures," he reminded them, "Thus it is written, that the Messiah is to suffer and to rise from the dead on the third day, and that *repentance and forgiveness of sins is to be proclaimed in his name to all nations*, beginning from Jerusalem" (24:46-47, NRSV, emphasis added).

Luke, of course, tells many of the same stories of healing recorded in the other Gospels. However, only he tells a number of healing incidents in which the identity of the recipient seems highlighted. These people are on the periphery of Jewish society.

Only Luke tells of the Gentile centurion's slave being healed (7:1-10). Only Luke mentions that Joanna and Susanna, women likely known to the church, were among those Jesus had cured (8:1-2). Then there are the stories only Luke mentions about the crippled woman (13:10-17), the man with dropsy (14:1-6), and the ten lepers from Samaria and Galilee who were cured (17:11-19).

Only Luke tells the story of the street woman who anointed Jesus' feet. She was forgiven because "She has loved much." To this burdened woman, who must have been an example of many women in the church, Jesus said, "Your sins are forgiven. . . . Your faith has saved you; go in peace" (7:36-50). Only Luke records the parables of the prodigal son (15:11-32) and the Pharisee and publican (18:9-14), and the story of Zacchaeus, the tax collector (19:1-10). In 17:3-4 Luke records a warning of Jesus about personal offenses that break fellowship and the strategic importance of forgiveness as the solution.

To this we can add the significant way in which Luke underscores the importance of forgiveness in his carefully selected version of Matthew's "Sermon on the Mount." He begins, like Matthew, with the characteristics of true disciples (6:20-26), then follows immediately with an extended section on loving enemies, forgiveness, and dealing with fellow disciples (27-42). This in essence makes up the so-called "Sermon on the Plain."

When we remember that Luke is writing in the context of and for the admonition of the early church, it seems significant that he should have underscored this aspect of Jesus' mission as precedent for the life of the church. Clearly for Luke also, the church is the healing, reconciling community of the Spirit.

John

The Fourth Gospel has often been viewed as a more mystical work which speaks to the individual's union with Christ. Different commentators have noted that *ekklēsia* nor the concept of the "people of God" occur in the book.[9] Rudolf Schnackenburg, who has written a three-volume commentary on *John*, writes,

> The impression that is given in the Gospel, then, is that it presents an individual view and does not emphasize the idea of community. This is, however, a deceptive impression. . . . Johannine Christianity is no different from the rest of early Christianity in that it was convinced that Christian existence could not be realized outside or without community (1990: 209).

Newton Flew (along with many commentators since), points out that both the image of the shepherd and flock, as well as of the vine and the branches, allude to Israel as God's flock and "the vine of David" (1943:172-173). Thus such imagery points to the church rather than individuals. The reference to a community of disciples is explicit when Jesus as the Good Shepherd says that there will be "one flock, [with] one shepherd" as a result of his sacrificial death (10:16).

In his high priestly prayer Jesus prayed for the unity of the whole body of disciples in God as he found his own life and fellowship in union with the Father (17:21). This oneness of the church in the Father and the Son is to be their "glory"—their identifying characteristic (v. 22).

Thus we conclude that this "most spiritual Gospel" also speaks of the church as the continuing body through which the Spirit of Christ is made manifest to the world. Earlier this century E. F. Scott put it well.

John accepts in a yet fuller and more literal sense the idea
of Ephesians, that the Church is the body of Christ—the
vesture of flesh which the eternal Word is always renewing in order to abide with men for ever. . . . The community of the disciples, as the germinal Church, is to replace
Christ after he is gone, and to manifest him as still present
(Macgregor, 1929:320).

Further, as in the other Gospels, John's description
of the ministry of Jesus "prefigured and anticipated the
life and experience of the church" (Klassen and Snyder, 1962:127). The events and words of the earthly Jesus recalled by John seem clearly selected and edited
to speak to the church situation in which he was writing. Not only individual incidents, but the whole pattern of Jesus' life and ministry, prefigure the life of the
church in the world. Nils Dahl, whom we quoted
above, wrote, "The ministry of Jesus in Israel, his voluntary death as 'king of the Jews,' and his glorification
by God are, thus, the historical and juridical basis for
the life of the church and for witness which it brings to
all men [sic]" (1962:139).

According to the Gospel of John the church is a community of believers. They are a community formed by
the word of God which has enlightened them (Flew,
1943:177f.). Like the blind man in John 9, they are
those who have received their sight and openly confess Jesus to be the Christ.

Schnackenburg notes that the word disciple
(*mathētēs*) is used seventy-eight times by John, more
than in any other Gospel. But John defines disciples as
those who have come to belief through Jesus' signs
and words. To follow Jesus means to "walk in the

light" (8:12).[10] To "walk in the light" means to openly confess Jesus as the truth of God and to live in obedience to him.

This church of believers is a community of those who share in the Spirit of Christ. They exist as a "fellowship" (koinonia) of those who know the love of God and express it in their lives. They live and walk in the light. The Spirit guides them into all truth of Christ (16:13-15). This essential characteristic separates them from the "world" of darkness, fear, and hostility. They are a community of those "born of the Spirit" (1:13) through whom God's love is made known in the world.

John describes the church as organically and personally related to Christ. It is a *sacramental* community. This means that through the indwelling life of Christ's Spirit it embodies him in the world. Having been born anew by the Spirit of God, its members live by the spiritual nourishment ("eating and drinking") which Christ's body and blood provide (3:5-6; 6:53).

They live as branches given life by vital connection to the vine (15:4). Their definition and unity as a community of Christ depends entirely on their participation in the life of the Father and the Son (17:21). They are the continuing sign of the presence of Christ through the Spirit which has been given them (17:26; 20:23).

The church is the sign of Christ's continuing presence in the world and precipitates *crisis* just as Jesus did. If it is truly living in the light and bearing witness to the truth, it becomes the instrument through which the Spirit convicts the world of its sin and injustice

(15:26-27; 16:8-11). It creates a situation in which decision and judgment must be made. Those who decide against the light and truth in Jesus, condemn themselves (3:18-19).

Thus in words reminiscent of Matthew 18, the Spirit's presence in the church makes its witness a source and standard for forgiveness and (self-)judgment. However, in distinction from Matthew, the church is not given *authority* ("keys") to forgive or retain sins. Rather, by the living presence of the Spirit in its midst, its message becomes the catalyst of judgment (15:22).

The church is the servant community. As servants of the Master Servant, Jesus' disciples are to follow his example of washing each other's feet (13:1-17). Theirs is not a mission of domination and power, but of service and suffering. They live in the world as sheep in the midst of wolves, defenseless and totally dependent on God for protection. In this they follow the example of their Master (15:18-21; 17:15). As the "Son of man" was "glorified" by being lifted up on the cross, so all those who serve him must follow him in suffering and death (12:26).[11]

Finally, John clearly indicates that the church's mission is worldwide. To begin with, he sets Christ's ministry in "the world," not Israel. This world is both the object of God's mission, and the hostile opposition to Christ. The "Jews," the opponents of Jesus, are a representative part of this world, in both senses of the word. Indeed, they are portrayed as "the concentrated expression" of the antagonism to Jesus.

Nils Dahl points out that the author of the Fourth

Gospel assumes the perspective of the Jews themselves, namely, "that Israel is the center of the world." This implies, on the one hand, that "the mission of Jesus in Israel is a mission to the world and that he fulfilled his ministry to the world within Israel. Negatively, it means that the world's enmity and opposition to God gets its concentrated expression through the Jews" (Klassen, 1962:129). Thus John's Gospel should not be read as an anti-Semitic polemic against Judaism. It is rather a penetrating description of the crisis which the light of Christ causes in the world.

The Gospel begins with the "Word" which created the world and has been the continuing light and life of the world (1:1-5). This Word as the "Son of God" was sent into the world to save it (3:16ff.). In contrast to the "Jews" the Samaritans accept his claim to be the Messiah and confess their faith that this one "is indeed the Savior of the world" (4:39-42).

Again, Jesus is reported to have said, "I have other sheep that do not belong to this fold. I must bring them also, and they will listen to my voice" (10:16, NRSV). This seems clearly to refer to those beyond the fold of Israel. And, finally, it is John who notes that the inscription put above Jesus' head on the cross was written "in Hebrew, in Latin, and in Greek" (19:20).

In 12:20ff. Philip and Andrew introduce Greek visitors to Jesus, who then uses the setting to predict his approaching crucifixion and the dissemination of his movement. Dahl has called this "the great mission text" of John. "The coming of the Greeks, who wish to see Jesus, is a sign that 'the hour has come for the Son of man to be glorified.' His earthly ministry in Israel has come to an end; the universal mission is to be inaugurated by the death of Jesus. . ." (1962:126).[12]

Jesus and the Church[13]

What, then, may we conclude was the role of Jesus in the emergence of the church? We have seen that all the authors of the Gospels assume and imply what Luke makes explicit by writing a Gospel in two acts—that Jesus as the Messiah was "pioneer and perfecter" of the church's life and message. For Luke the nucleus of the new community is the continuation and expansion of the original twelve. The 120 disciples (Acts 1:15) of Jesus, who waited in prayer for the next move of the risen Christ, are the completion of the symbolic number of apostles.

Raymond Brown has noted that Luke

made a bold ecclesial step when he enlarged the story of Jesus' ministry and death which Mark 1:1 called "the gospel of Jesus Christ," not only by rewriting and developing the Jesus story, but also by adding a second book concerning early Christianity. He was putting together on the same level the story of the proclamation of the kingdom by Jesus and the story of the proclamation of Jesus by Peter and Paul. This means that the good news or gospel concerns not only what God has done in Jesus but also what He has done in the Spirit (1984:64).

As we have seen, both Matthew and John implicitly also make these same connections.

We have noted the way in which the Gospels indicate the historical and theological relation between the ministry of Jesus and that of the church. Now we will summarize how Jesus is connected to what comes after his historical presence.

First, Jesus is the *historical source* of the new movement. Purely on a historical level it is inconceivable, as Sean Freyne has observed,

> that the later Christian movement based on belief in Jesus' name could have been thought of let alone succeed, were it not for the fact that there was an actual historical contribution from those who were followers of Jesus during his lifetime (1980:136).

Jesus did not organize the church during his earthly ministry. The church as it emerges in the New Testament was not possible prior to Jesus' death, resurrection, and the manifestation of the Holy Spirit as the messianic blessing. But that does not rule out an authentic, historical relation between the mission of the earthly Jesus and the emerging church. Neither does it imply that he had no vision of community as a goal of his mission.

As has often been pointed out, the concept of a Messiah without a community of followers is not possible. Jesus as the Messiah was forming a new and renewed Israel, which "the twelve" symbolized. He provided a new covenant, taught a new ethic, and gave a new commission to this eschatological community we call church.[14]

The church is not the creation of Jesus' followers, who conceived a mythical "Christ of faith" and made him the focus of a new religious sect. Neither is it an afterthought in the plan of God for the salvation of the world. It is both a genetic and intrinsic outcome of the life and ministry of Jesus.

Schnackenburg puts it well.

> The community contained in the bosom of Judaism and then emerging from it cannot be understood without the coming and work of Jesus of Nazareth. It continues on a new plane that movement of assembly which he had begun with his message of the approaching kingdom of God. Consequently the interest of the primitive Church in the Jesus of history was a living and indispensable one . . . (1965:13).

Second, Jesus is the *theological ground* of the new community. The conviction that God had vindicated Jesus as the Messiah by raising him from death lay at the inception of the church's development. This conviction sustained the 120 disciples who continued to meet in the temple. It was the first theological announcement of the church at Pentecost (Acts 2:36) and identified them as a distinctive group within Judaism and later as a separate movement.

The understanding of his messianic role developed slowly. Apparently at first the church associated it with his apocalyptic return to establish an earthly reign. They were greatly disappointed when he was executed (Luke 24:21), but they came to view his earthly ministry and death as a preparation for his imminent return and reign as the Messiah.

Thus they formed a network of apostolic communities still attached to the Jewish temple, waiting for him to return and establish the kingdom he had announced (Acts 1:6). All the while they were spreading the word that Jesus was indeed God's Messiah. This is the picture we get from Acts 2—4.

Along with the conviction that Jesus was the messianic "Son of God" (John 20:31) and "Savior of the world" (John 4:42), his disciples adopted his message of the "kingdom of God" as their own. The newly formed movement understood its mission as the proclamation of this "gospel of the kingdom."

In its most rudimentary terms, the kingdom of God means simply the recognition of God's authority or rule in the affairs of humankind. It means the presence and authority of God precisely as taught and demonstrated in the life of Jesus of Nazareth. It means casting out fear, shame, and evil; the forgiveness of sins; and immediate access to God as one of his children. It means bread and justice for the poor and oppressed. It is that happy state of affairs under the blessing of God for which Jesus taught his disciples to pray when they said, "Your kingdom come, your will be done on earth as it is in heaven" (Matt. 6:10, NIV).

This concept of God's kingship was not a new creation, either of Jesus or the church. Judaism had long taught that God is king (Ps. 74:12). They had understood salvation as both an individual and social reality in which God's people live in *shalom* (peace) under his rule. New was the conviction that the resurrected Jesus is the one who exercises God's authority.

Jesus has been "exalted at the right hand of God" (Acts 2:33). Not the temple authorities nor the scribes who guarded the tradition of Moses, but Jesus of Nazareth is the authentic witness to the nature of God's rule. It was this basic theological conviction that caused the final division between Judaism and the Christian church.

By the time most of the Gospels were written, the expectation that Jesus would return to establish a political kingdom in the immediate future had been modified. His followers began to understand that the pre-resurrection Christ had already introduced the kingdom of God. They began to interpret his death as a vicarious sacrifice establishing a new covenant people of God. They realized that his resurrection not only vindicated his claim to be the future Messiah, it validated his understanding of his messianic role as suffering servant. The "kingdom" he had inaugurated was a present transcendent possibility for all who would "enter" it (Mark 3:23-27). The earthly Jesus already was the Messiah, and the church was his continuing representative proclaiming the kingdom of God.

That meant Jesus' message and way of life, radical as they were, had been validated by God. Thus, in the third place, Jesus is related to the church as *its exemplar*. The kingdom of God does not lie in some near or distant *parousia* (coming). It is in the midst of the community (Luke 17:20). This community in which the kingdom of God is coming is to put the kingdom and its values first (Matt. 6:33). It is to be governed by the *agape* commandment (Matt. 22:37-39; John 13:34-35).

Jesus' followers are to preach the "gospel of the kingdom" that the God of Jesus Christ is totally available to all who submit to his rule. And as kingdom centers they are to be "the light of the world" and "the salt of the earth" (Matt. 5:13-16). Thus the community that formed attempted to live out the implications of their confession that Jesus was the Messiah.

Martin Hengel suggests also that Jesus established a model for the church as a missionary movement (1983:62-63). He calls Jesus the "primal missionary." The text for such a concept is, of course, John 17:18. Jesus established and defined the mission and its goal. According to Matthew 28:19-20, the disciples are to do exactly what Jesus himself did, under his authority. They are to go out "in his name" with the keys to unlock the kingdom. And following him as "pioneer," they may expect the same treatment he received (Luke 21:16-17; John 15:18; 16:2-3).

Finally, Jesus is related to the church as its *enlivening spirit and continuing leader*. Each of the Gospel writers affirm this in their own way. According to Matthew, Jesus promises always to be among the gathered community (18:20; 28:20). According to Luke, he sends his Spirit, who takes charge of the mission (Acts 2:33). According to John, he himself returns in the mode of Spirit (14:16-18). There is no reference to Jesus' continuing presence in the body of the Gospel of Mark, but the longer ending reports that "the Lord worked with them and confirmed the message. . . ."

This living presence or Spirit of Christ is the catalyst uniting the church with God its source. It is the Power which motivates and activates the church for its mission. It is the Wisdom that leads the church into truth as it attempts to understand its role in the world. It is the Spirit that guarantees its continuing authenticity and authority as the "body of Christ." In short, Jesus is the abiding presence apart from which the church has no genuine identity as the messianic movement.

4

The Apostolic Community

The Christian Church was born as a *mission to the world*. It was apostolic—sent into the world with a divine commission. That apostolic character is of its essence.[1] If we may carry the imagery of birth further, we might say that the first cry of life from the newborn church was the proclamation that Jesus is Lord of heaven and earth as well as Messiah of the Jews (Acts 2:36).

The proclamation that Jesus is Lord and the formation of a new community had an inseparable organic relation to each other. Word and event together were the proclamation of the new thing God's Spirit was doing among humankind. Proclaimed was the resurrection and victory of Jesus, the Messiah. Historically demonstrated was a new community characterized by the Spirit of Jesus—the spirit of love and hope.

Jesus' lordship was given form in the new resurrection community. Thus the reality of the new community was itself part of the proclamation. If the words about the historical Jesus or the ideal he portrayed are separated from the power and spirit of the living Christ made present in an actual community of redemption, they cannot be properly understood.

The proclamation in word and deed that "Jesus is

Lord" was directed outward to the world. Jesus' disciples were to be witnesses "to the end of the earth." They announced that the "kingdom/rule of God" had arrived and was destined to cover the earth and include all its people.

This outward directedness gave the new community the characteristics of a movement.[2] The early Christians did not announce the formation of a new religious society gathered out of the larger social order to nourish and sustain itself as a community of faith. They joined the new movement to be part of God's mission to the world, not to escape the world or to set up some island of security in it.

Thus the life of the first community was open to the world and by intention included the world. What was done in the community was a sign and invitation to others to participate in the new reality God had created by the Spirit of Christ.

The life and character of the new community were integral and essential to its witness. This point cannot be overemphasized today![3] The new spirit and practice of selfless sharing (*koinonia*) was central in the community life. This was the Spirit made present in Jesus' followers. To be saved meant to participate in this new social reality created by the Spirit of Christ and offered to the world. Even so, the apostles refused to accept responsibility for the organization and administration of this essential community function (Acts 6:2-4). This refusal has crucial significance for our understanding of the church and its mission.

The apostles have often been criticized for appointing deacons, or helpers, to administer relief and aid to the needy while they concentrated on prayer and preaching. This is a case of misplaced spirituality, the indictment runs. The apostles did not see the holistic relation between the physical, social, and spiritual. Their critics claim that the apostles failed to understand the profound significance of the new koinonia reality which had emerged among them.

On the other hand, some modern evangelical commentators have lauded this apostolic action as a precedent which establishes the priority of the spiritual ministry of the word (preaching) over social service in the mission of the church. Both arguments miss the larger, central point implicit in the apostles' action.

The apostles bore in their calling and function the essential character of the new movement. Apostles are not in essence administrators of a religious society. They are messengers divinely commissioned to lead a movement. The church is in essence the apostolic movement. That is why the apostles delegated this important but nevertheless secondary organizational responsibility to helpers. Had they accepted the role of administrators of internal affairs in the community, they would have subverted the integrity of the mission. Care for the needy was an essential part of the new community, but the community was not a relief and social services society.

The complaint of the Hellenists was itself an implicit denial of the inclusive, open character of the new movement. They had already begun to think of the movement as a religious society or sect organized to meet their needs, and undoubtedly many of the other converts likewise misunderstood.

The significance of this story about internal difficulty (6:1-6) should be understood in light of the prior incident involving Ananias and Sapphira (5:1-11). The hypocrisy of Ananias and Sapphira threatened the integrity of the koinoniac character of the mission. The Hellenists' complaint threatened the integrity of the mission character of the koinonia community. If the apostles had assumed the role of mutual aid administrators, they would have encouraged this misunderstanding. Within an apostolic (missionary) context, koinonia is itself part of the mission. Outside that apostolic context sharing becomes exclusive and sectarian.

The nature of the new community of the Spirit cannot be defined or understood apart from its being a witness to the lordship of Jesus Christ. In his book *The Nature and Mission of the Church*, Donald G. Miller quotes Emil Brunner as saying, "The church exists by mission as fire exists by burning" (1957:69)! This is a happy metaphor in many ways.

The "Gospel of the Kingdom"

For over a century now Bible and prophetic conferences have rung the changes on the relation of the "kingdom" and the "church" in New Testament interpretations. This argument is important chiefly because it impinges directly on the practical matters of the mission strategy of the church. What is the character of the church's mission in the world? How does it relate to everyday "secular" life and social structure? What is the Holy Spirit's role in all of this? How does the Spirit's presence relate to church activity on the one hand and secular activity on the other? What is the purpose and goal of the church's mission?

It is unnecessary for our discussion of these questions to enter into the more minuscule aspects of the long, ponderous, and sometimes tiresome debate about the order of events in God's plan for the consummation of history. However, we do need to examine those larger aspects of the discussion which have a direct bearing on the nature of the present mission and strategy of the apostolic community.

The deep concern of J. N. Darby and his associates about the condition of Christendom, and their convictions about the nature of the true church, were what initially gave rise to the dispensationalist debate about prophecy. Much current evangelical terminology and debate about such issues as "postponement of the kingdom," "secret rapture," and the nature of the millennium hinge on the nature of the apostolic mission of the church.[4] Our concern in this chapter remains this initial and primary question—namely, the nature of the church.

The discussion of New Testament interpretation has revolved around whether the kingdom of God/heaven has already come to be through the resurrection of Christ and the formation of the church, or whether it has been postponed to a future fulfillment with the church as an interim arrangement.[5] How does the church relate to the ultimate goal of God in redeeming humankind and establishing the kingdom of righteousness?

The phrase "kingdom of God/heaven," is found largely in the synoptic Gospels, where it is attributed to Jesus himself. Luke continues to use the phrase in

Acts when he reports Paul's sermons, and there are scattered references in the Pauline letters and the general epistles. But the term is by no means so central in the epistles as in the synoptic Gospels. This rather striking shift in terminology has been offered by dispensationalist scholars as conclusive evidence that the church is something other than and quite distinct from the kingdom.

According to C. I. Scofield, whom many evangelical teachers follow, "rightly dividing the Word" means applying the epistles to the church age and most of the synoptic Gospels to the kingdom. According to this interpretation, Jesus offered the Jews an earthly fulfillment of the kingdom but withdrew the offer when they rejected him as their Messiah. Instead of a present earthly kingdom, Jesus founded the church to preach the gospel of salvation through Jesus' sacrificial death, and to prepare individuals to enter the future kingdom.

The kingdom is viewed as a distinct future era or "dispensation" in God's unfolding plan for history. It will be brought in through the political dominion of Christ when he returns to the earth. This "kingdom" is generally identified with the millennial reign of Christ. The church's mission meanwhile is only indirectly related to the goals of the kingdom of God. Its mission is the salvation of individuals from a doomed world so they may participate in the future kingdom.

Whether or not they subscribe to the finer points of dispensationalist eschatology, most fundamentalist and evangelical Bible teachers and preachers do accept this theological view of church and kingdom. They

model their congregational life and witness accordingly. They understand the mission of the church to be
primarily the evangelistic preaching of the gospel and
the saving of souls.

The Kingdom and the Church

Both the centrality of Pentecost to the gospel, and the
continuity of the apostolic mission with that of Jesus
himself, raise questions about this view of radical discontinuity between the church and kingdom. Those
who first followed the risen Christ thought and spoke
of themselves as a movement under a new messianic
ruler. Such an appeal obviously evokes kingdom im-
ages! On the day of Pentecost, for example, Peter proclaimed Jesus "Lord and Messiah" and called his audience to leave their old "generation" and pledge allegiance to Jesus as the authority in the new community.
This implies far more than the evangelistic call to individual sinners to get right with God.

Further, Luke represents Paul as preaching the
"kingdom of God" in his ministry to the Gentiles; and
Paul's use of the phrase in his epistles indicates that
Luke has correctly represented him. Yet it is obvious
that the term is not so central for Paul as for Jesus. How
then are we to account for the shift in terminology
from "kingdom" to "church" in the New Testament itself? And what does it imply about the apostles' self-
understanding of their mission?

We begin with brief comments to clarify the issues,
and postpone elaboration of the meaning of the kingdom of God to the next chapter. Here the question is
the relation of kingdom and church as it bears on the

mission and strategy of the church. (The order of discussion is dictated more by the historical circumstance of the debate than by logical order.)

The kingdom of God means God's saving, governing presence. That rule has both a present and a future aspect. Where God is present in saving power, where his authority is acknowledged and his will done on earth, there his kingdom becomes present. Even now men and women enter that kingdom, and such citizens of the kingdom have eternal life. The kingdom is among us as a miraculous gift of God, but even as we acknowledge its presence we pray it may come in its consummate fullness—"on earth as it is in heaven."

It is this dual nature of the kingdom as already present in power but not definable as a realm or political institution that raises the question of the church's relation to it. The church is not the kingdom. Yet it proclaims the good news of the kingdom, and the "keys of the kingdom" have been entrusted to it.

The typical evangelical Protestant solution is to relegate the kingdom to the realm of "spiritual" and individual experience. For example, George Eldon Ladd, whose book, *The Gospel of the Kingdom*, is a very helpful interpretation of many aspects of the kingdom, explains the "mystery of the kingdom" as follows.

What Jesus meant is this, "Yes, the Kingdom of God is here. But there is a mystery—a new revelation about the Kingdom. The Kingdom of God is here; but instead of destroying human sovereignty, it has attacked the sovereignty of Satan. The Kingdom of God is here; but instead of making changes in the external, political order of things, it is making changes in the spiritual order and in the lives of men and women" (1971:55).

This solution seems to limit the power and scope of the kingdom to the internal experience of individuals. It does not do justice to the New Testament view of the centrality of the church in God's plan for the salvation of the world. In his article on "*Basileus* and Its Correlates in the New Testament" Karl Schmidt observes that in the case of Jesus and his apostles "it is not the individual as such who receives the promises, but only the congregation, as a member of which the individual receives salvation" (Kittel, 1964:586).

We could here substitute the word "kingdom" for "salvation." The kingdom is manifest as the rule of Christ in the church, and individuals experience that saving rule as they participate in the "community of the king."[6]

The New Testament word for church or congregation is *ekklēsia*, which literally means "assembly." Following the analogy of the imperial colonies throughout the Roman Empire, the word is often used to indicate the assemblies or centers of God's kingdom, such as the assemblies at Thessalonica, Philippi, and Corinth. It is also used in the singular to indicate the unity of the movement under its one Lord—that is, the church throughout the world. This latter usage, however, is far less common than the first.

Paul specifically used the metaphor of a Roman colony to describe the Christian center at Philippi (Phil. 3:20). The city itself was such a colony or military outpost of the Roman government.[7] Just so, the congregation was an outpost of God's kingdom ruled from heaven. From Paul's letter we learn that this small outpost was withstanding heavy attack for their aggressive promotion of the gospel. Indeed, Paul himself is writing from jail, where he is under indictment for subversion of the Roman government. Nevertheless, his main concern is the advance of the cause. He urges party unity and team spirit as Christians strive shoulder to shoulder for the gospel faith. The political imagery is obvious. This is kingdom talk!

The concept of God's kingdom is also implicit in the many references to Jesus as Lord and head of the church. In the Gospels, Jesus' presence and message are virtually equated with the presence of the kingdom of God. In Luke 11:20 and its parallels, for example, Jesus' ministry of casting out demons is proclaimed as an immediate manifestation of the kingdom. The Palm Sunday crowds hailed the entry of Jesus into Jerusalem as the entry of the king "who comes in the name of the Lord," and as the coming of the kingdom of David (Mark 11:9-10).

Again in Luke 18:29 and parallels, Jesus' "name," the "gospel," and the "kingdom of God" are used synonymously. This kind of easy parallelism suggests that the church closely associated the presence of the Spirit of Christ and the presence of the kingdom of God. Its recognition that the redeeming rule of God had broken uniquely into history in Jesus Christ was proclaimed in its confession that Jesus is Lord.

In the closing paragraph of his more detailed review of this kind of New Testament data, Schmidt concludes, "It is not the case that the emphasis on the

Church has supplanted Jesus of Nazareth's preaching of the Kingdom of God. Rather it is the case that in the post-Easter experience of Christ the belief in the Kingdom of God remained firm" (Kittel, 1964:589).

The use of new terminology can be accounted for most simply by the observation that "kingdom of God" is a colloquial Jewish expression that needed translation in the Gentile setting. *Ekklēsia* was an indigenous Hellenistic term with political overtones that made it acceptable as a translation of terms like "people," "synagogue," or "kingdom of God." It did not in the first instance have the connotation of a religious society. Further, *ekklēsia* was a far more concrete word to use in referring to the multiplying centers throughout the Roman Empire.

It seems unnecessary, therefore, to elaborate a complex theory of discontinuity between church and kingdom which involves God in a major strategy change to account for the shift in terminology. Furthermore, such a theory makes the church peripheral to God's plan of salvation in a way that is quite foreign to the New Testament.

To be sure, there were changes in the life of the church as Christianity became predominantly a Gentile movement. The understanding of Christ's relation to the churches was spiritualized with the passing of time and the change of cultural context. The concept of Jesus as a Jewish political messiah was modified. A shift in emphasis from proclamation (*kerygma*) to moral teaching (*didachē*) also seems to have occurred, as relatively more elementary explanation was required for the new recruits.

Then too, the apostles seem to have become progressively aware that their mission would not be triumphantly consummated in the immediate future. (They apparently clung for a while to the hope of an immediate restoration of political authority to Israel in spite of Jesus' disclaimer.) Such changes, however, do not necessarily indicate that the church understood itself to be only peripherally related to the kingdom of God.

The Nature of Apostolic Mission

We can strengthen the argument for a strategic relation between the kingdom and the church by noting the way in which the New Testament speaks about the end of history. It speaks of the end as both the fulfillment of historical experience (*parousia*) and a further revelation (*epiphania*). It is both *climax* to what has preceded and the *inauguration* of a new era. In this respect the second advent parallels the first.

Note that two things are said in this affirmation. To speak of the end as climax or consummation is to relate it to the historical chain of events which precede it. The end does not come as a tour de force—an arbitrary act of power canceling what has preceded. It comes as a *fulfillment* of the mission of the church in history. The further manifestation will simply be a fuller disclosure of "this same Jesus" (Acts 1:11, NIV). That is why the future presence (*parousia*) must be called the *second* advent.

But while the end is climactic, it is also the initiation of what is new and different. This final manifestation (*epiphania*) presents us with more than the cumulative effects of the activity of the "church militant." It will be a new, decisive manifestation of Christ's lordship as "King of kings, and Lord of lords."

The classic Augustinian model of church and kingdom, sometimes called postmillennialism, did not adequately recognize the new aspect of the second advent. This weakness was especially evident in its modern, liberal, evolutionary formulation.

A significant advance in God's plan for history has been inaugurated by Jesus in his first advent. The commission for carrying out this phase of the operation under his own leadership has been given to the apostolic community—the church.[8] To use a parallel from Israel's history, the Jordan River has been crossed, the troops assigned, and the conquest of Canaan begun.

This is the central message of Ephesians, which unfolds the "mystery" of God's plan for history. The author first states that the disclosure was made "in Christ" (1:9). Christ has broken down the old ethnic and religious barriers between Jewish Israel and the nations (2:14). He is the "chief cornerstone" (NIV) in the new structure being built as a "dwelling place of God in the Spirit" (2:19-22).

The content of the mystery which is unfolded turns out to be precisely the message of Pentecost—namely, that membership in the community of the Spirit has been extended universally through the good news. The nations are being offered a share in the fulfillment of "the promise in Christ Jesus through the gospel" (3:1-6). Further, this new phase, elsewhere referred to as "the rule of God," is being demonstrated (made known) to the cosmic powers and authorities *through the church* (3:7-13).

Both Paul and Luke give a central place to the church and its apostolic mission as the spearhead of the kingdom. Lampe has pointed out that of all the Gospels, Luke emphasizes the significance of the church in the further advance of the kingdom of God. Lampe notes the explicit parallels between Jesus' messianic mission through the power of the Spirit and the continuation of that same mission by the disciples, who receive a baptism of the Spirit for mission (1955:168, 194). This does not mean that the disciples, as agents of the Holy Spirit, bring in the kingdom. It does, however, indicate that the work of the disciples is kingdom work.

For Paul the church is in the center of God's plan for advancing the gospel of the kingdom. Paul presents himself as the commissioned representative of the "Lord" and the apostolic community. He is Christ's ambassador to the Gentiles, offering them a place in the new reality God is creating. And he calls them to become part of the church—the "new humanity," the "new commonwealth," the "household of God"—which has been commissioned to make known or demonstrate the "gospel of peace" to the fragmented, hostile powers of this age.

There is only one gospel of Christ, and it is the "gospel of the kingdom." Christ is both message and the messenger. As message he is the one in whom the authoritative presence and power of God unto salvation becomes reality. As messenger he proclaims the rule or kingdom of God—announcing that in a decisive, new way God's presence and power are manifest among us.

The church has been commissioned to advance this

good news with all its attending implications. As the anticipatory manifestation of the kingdom, it calls humankind to accept the authority of God, which means to "enter the kingdom." Claude Welch has written, "The church is always 'for a purpose,' and the final end of its being is always God and his Kingdom" (1958:211).

Movement or Society?

For the lay reader the New Testament language in the standard translations has almost become jargon. It is filled with specialized terms which do not denote familiar, everyday meanings. This unfortunate circumstance has led to the many translations which have flooded the market in recent years.

For example, what does the term "kingdom of heaven" mean to most contemporary Christians? By and large those I have questioned simply take it as a synonym of heaven. This has led to much ambiguity and misunderstanding of the issues. All of us are familiar with the almost universal Sunday school question whether rich people can go to heaven when they die. But Jesus was not speaking primarily of a rich person's future destiny. It was the rich person's availability now, as follower and disciple, that concerned Jesus.

In the early 1960s, Clarence Jordan, founder of Koinonia Farm, was making a colloquial paraphrase of the New Testament. He was searching for a term to translate the phrase "kingdom of God." What modern term would convey the implications and feelings which the phrase stirred up in the mind of the first-century Jew? Well aware of the newly emerging civil rights movement in the African-American churches of the South, he hit on the happy phrase "the God Movement." Thus according to Jordan's translation Jesus came preaching that the God Movement was about to begin.[9]

Through these terms we can see in a new light the issues at stake in the argument about the relation of the kingdom of heaven and the church. The question now becomes whether the church is a vital part of the God Movement.[10] Is the church merely another religious society or club which provides its members the special privileges of club membership? Is it an interim missionary society organized for recruiting new members while we wait for the reintroduction of the God Movement at some auspicious moment in the future?

Or is the church an integral, functioning part of a movement successfully launched by the Christ whose Spirit now directs it? Today it almost seems incredible that anyone would ever have equated the institutional church with the God Movement, as some Christians did in a more optimistic age. But is it not a vital part of the Movement?

Perhaps this is the place to pause and look further at the significance of describing the church as a movement rather than a religious society. The word movement suggests dynamism and action. A movement forms as a consequence of powerful convictions or events which call for action and change in response. Mission, not organizational structure, gives cohesiveness and form to a movement. Organization is secondary and determined by the nature of the mission which actually forms the movement.

An even more fundamental characteristic of a movement is its dynamic and open relationship to the larger social order in which it operates. A movement seeks to bring about change in the social order. It tries to turn the direction of historical development. Thus it does not understand itself as a separate or peripheral subculture but as a force for change within the dominant culture.[11]

According to the New Testament, this is the nature of the God Movement. It does not have organizationally defined boundaries. Jesus likened it to yeast in dough, to salt in food, to light shining in the dark, and to a seed that grows into a tree.

It is this dynamic movement of God in and for the world that provides the context for all the life and work of the church—whether it be evangelism, education, mutual aid, or social service. Let us look more carefully at implications of this way of viewing the church.

Church Membership and the God Movement

First, when the church is defined as movement, the requirements for membership will be support of the goals and methods of the God Movement. The criterion for belonging is commitment to the Christ as leader of the movement. The password is "Christ is Lord." This commitment is more important than agreement with correct theological formulas, a qualifying religious experience, or assent to a particular moral discipline. Loyalty, trust, and serious involvement are key in a movement.

cal grounds, today others within the evangelical persuasion are challenging the older theological position
from within. They base their challenge in the Bible.[2]

Why the conflict? Evangelicalism has always made
peace a central word in its message of salvation. The
classical message of evangelicalism is that by the sacrifice of Christ we have been justified and forgiven
through faith. Our sins have been removed as a cause
of God's anger; our feelings of uneasiness and guilt
have been lifted. Romans 5:1, "Therefore, since we are
justified by faith, we have peace with God through our
Lord Jesus Christ," was a central text of the Reformation. It has remained a favorite word of assurance and
comfort for countless thousands of anxious, burdened
individuals who have "made peace with God."

But what has this to do with war, riots, and violent
revolutions against political oppressors? Should
Christians expect and work for peace *in the world*, or is
the message of peace with God only one of inner, spiritual tranquility in the midst of confusion and violence? What did Jesus mean when he told his anxious
followers, "My peace I give to you" (John 14:27)? To
understand the nature and significance of the dispute
and to find answers to such questions, we need both
the perspective of history and a clearer understanding
of biblical concepts.

"Peace with God"

During the revivals of the early 1800s, individuals in
great inner conflict and fear due to sin often struggled
for days in a state of depression and anxiety before
they were able to "pray through" and gain peace of

mind. From this tradition, which has colored so much of our religious vocabulary, "peace with God" has come to be practically equated with justification and assurance of salvation.

Theologically, peace has come to mean that the guilt of sin has been properly settled (justification) through the substitutionary penalty paid by Jesus on the cross. Psychologically, it means that the anxiety feelings of guilt have been resolved, the burden of shame has been lifted, and a sense of assurance and peace attained. However, the accentuation of guilt as the central problem in salvation must be traced still further back in the history of Christian thought.[3]

Already in the second and third centuries one can trace different interpretations of the atonement developing between the theologians in the Western, or Latin, tradition and those conditioned by the Hellenistic, or Greek, culture. Latin (Roman) theologians developed those biblical texts which view sin as transgression of law, and salvation as rescue from judgment and punishment. They were heavily influenced by Roman concepts and interpreted Christ's peacemaking as the "satisfaction of God's justice."

In the Greek Orthodox wing of the church, theologians stressed death as the consequences of sin and salvation as the gift of eternal life. The bread and wine of the Lord's Supper were called the "medicine of immortality." While these two emphases were not mutually exclusive, they produced quite different patterns of piety and theology.

By the tenth century, the two traditions had become fixed and largely separated. Concepts of punishment and just payment for sin were amplified to a high pitch within Roman Catholicism, which formed the context of the Protestant Reformation. God, and even Jesus, was pictured as a wrathful judge who condemned the wicked to endless torments of the inferno described so vividly by Dante. At best one could hope for an indeterminate sentence to purgatory. The whole ecclesiastical system of sacraments, pilgrimages, relics, and indulgences aimed at canceling temporal and eternal punishments by providing merits equivalent to the demerits of sin.

Luther reacted vigorously against the more legalistic aspects of this system in his search for personal salvation. Nevertheless he understood the basic problem as one of guilt and the just penalties involved. His struggle was for an inner assurance of God's forgiveness. He wanted a certainty of justification not dependent on any human individual or institution, not even the church. Thus the theological focus remained on sin as transgression of God's law, and on salvation as individual acquittal before God.

Luther thought he was simply reaffirming the message of Paul in Romans. But while he used Paul's words and in part captured his thought, Luther's accent falls on a different point than Paul's. He used Pauline vocabulary to speak to his own problem. The situation in which Paul was writing, and the problem that concerned him, were both different from Luther's. It is important to notice this difference because Luther's divergence from Paul was exaggerated and perpetuated by pietistic orthodoxy in the following centuries.

Luther was a medieval man trying to satisfy God,

whom he visualized as a stern and angry judge. In contrast, Paul said that even before his conversion he had a clear conscience before God. He was not in quest of personal peace and forgiveness, although when he discovered how wrong he had been, he too recognized that he was greatest of sinners.[4]

The great concern which filled Paul's mind was the relation of God to his people. As Paul the Pharisee understood the covenant law (Torah), God's peace and favor were conditioned on obedience to Torah. Israel was living in disobedience and so under the disfavor of God. As this young, fanatically loyal Jew saw it, the problem of restoration to God's favor and the key to messianic fulfillment was the problem of Israel's perfect obedience.

Then on the road to Damascus he came to the astonishing realization that the Messiah had indeed come, even though Israel had not rendered perfect obedience to Torah. Jesus of Nazareth whom he persecuted was the Messiah! And if the Messiah had come, then God had already intervened to bring peace to Israel—not because of the Jews' repentance and faithful obedience but in spite of their disobedience.

It was the implications of this discovery that Paul had to work through in the Arabian desert. God's peace comes to humankind as an act of *pure grace to be participated in through faith*. God did what Torah could not do because of humanity's weakness (Rom. 8:3-4). Because of this notable difference of personal and historical contexts, Paul's concept of "peace with God" is different from Luther's in significant ways.

Without developing the story in greater detail at this

point, we need simply note that Luther was the dominant figure in the Reformation, and he bequeathed an individualistic, spiritualized concept of peace to the Protestant tradition. Anabaptists like Pilgram Marpeck and Menno Simons were effectively silenced by persecution. Pietism, which claimed to be the legitimate spiritual heir to the Reformation, put singular emphasis on the individual experience of forgiveness, assurance, and the consequent response of personal holiness which should follow.

Today Protestant evangelicalism perpetuates this gospel of individualistic peace with God. The concept "peace of mind" has become so identified with the biblical message that the rich, multifaceted dimensions of the biblical meaning of peace have been largely overlooked.

Peace—Pax, Eirēnē, or Shalom?

Peace like heaven is highly desirable largely because the definition is so amenable to individual interpretation. For many peace means simply the absence of war or violence. Some make it almost synonymous with "law and order." Others think of it as freedom from anxiety and inner turmoil. And for still others it is the absence of confusion or tension in personal relationships. Peace means for them not having disagreements or showing anger.

These concepts derive from an ancient past. The Greeks thought of peace (eirēnē) as a kind of harmony or balance which resulted in stability. Peace was for them tranquillity. The ancient Romans from the time of Augustus referred to the Pax Romana (the peace of

Rome), which was maintained by the power of the emperor's troops. For them peace was a state of law and order.

In this cultural context, the New Testament writers spoke of Christ as the true "Prince of peace." God is "the God of peace," and the kingdom of God is a rule of peace. In its first century context Paul's statement that "the kingdom of God . . . [means] righteousness and peace and joy in the Holy Spirit" (Rom. 14:17) probably infers a contrast to the political peace of the Roman *pax*. Those motivated by the Spirit of peace "pursue what makes for peace and for mutual upbuilding" (v. 19). They do not need the coercion of laws and punitive discipline.

Although the New Testament was written in the cultural setting of the Roman Empire and in Greek words, the men who wrote it were of Hebrew background. They brought their own meanings to the words they used. It is almost as if they were translating their Hebrew ideas into Greek linguistic formulas. Because of this, it is necessary to look at the meaning of the word *shalom* in the Old Testament Scriptures to understand the meaning of writers like Peter and Paul. The "gospel of peace" is the gospel of shalom, not the gospel of the Greek *eirēnē* or the Roman *pax*.

According to the prophets, peace reigned in Israel when there was well-being, health, justice, equity, prosperity, and good will. Then the smile of God's favor was on the land. There was no peace if poverty, famine, or disease plagued the land. There was no peace when there was inequity in the distribution of wealth, injustice in the courts, or oppression of the poor. There was no peace when people forgot God and ignored his covenant law, which defined the order of peace and righteousness.

For example, Jeremiah described the plight of Israel torn by the sword of her enemies and decimated by plague and famine as the removal of God's peace from the people (16:5). He lamented that in this deplorable situation of greed, injustice, and impiety corrupt priests and prophets cry, " 'Peace, peace," when there is no peace" (6:14).

In the Hebrew Scriptures, then, peace is not simply relief from guilt feelings, serenity, or individual peace of mind. Shalom refers to harmonious social relationships which grow out of justice and equity in the public order.

This shalom is what God had prescribed in the covenant law. God's law is a "covenant of life and peace" (Mal. 2:5). Therefore, shalom in the public order is also understood as the relation between God and his people. Peace is the gift of God—a spiritual blessing, but having also political and economic as well as psychological and religious dimensions of meaning. It is a holistic concept and has come to be almost synonymous with salvation—seen as God's deliverance from evil, suffering, and sin. Peace is the fulfillment of the covenant promise, and it was this fulfillment to which Peter referred as "the gospel of peace" in his conversation with Cornelius (Acts 10:36).

This context provides a new perspective on the significance of Paul's words, "To set the mind on the flesh is death, but to set the mind on the Spirit is life and peace" (Rom. 8:6). The "mind set on the Spirit" fulfills the "covenant of life and peace" which God has made with his people.

The polarity here, as we noted in an earlier chapter, is between Spirit and law as the agent for accomplishing God's covenant purpose. Paul stated this quite explicitly in his letter to the Galatians (5:18). There he wrote, "But if you are led by the Spirit you are not under the law." To be "led by the Spirit" does not imply that peace has been spiritualized. Rather the Spirit's power furnishes a new possibility for peace to be realized in the covenant community. Peace is offered as a "fruit of the Spirit."

All this does not invalidate the concept of personal peace with God. Peace as reconciliation and inner confidence is a fundamental part of the biblical message. The inner freedom from conflict which comes through faith in Christ is a basic reality in the Christian's experience, and in fact is another facet of life in the Spirit. However, what we have observed in the preceding paragraphs is that peace cannot be equated simply with individual justification, freedom from guilt feelings, or inner tranquillity.

Peace, then, is a new state or quality of relationship with God and our fellow human beings. It is God's gift of the new possibility of community based on *agape* and bound together by his covenant of justice. It is not a human invention based on human justice and the legal regulation of individual self-interest. Thus when Israel stubbornly disobeyed God's covenant, Jeremiah said that God had removed his peace from them. Using the same idiom Jesus said, "My peace I give to you" (John 14:27). He said this in anticipation of the Spirit's coming and the disciples' obedience to his new covenant and commandment of love.

The Community of Peace

The gospel of peace announces the possibility of a new relationship with God, to be lived out in relation with our fellow human beings. It calls us to live for the God Movement, whose cause is "justice, peace, and joy, inspired by the Holy Spirit" (Rom. 14:17, NEB). This is the same message we earlier referred to as the good news of Pentecost—an announcement that a new community/movement of God's peace has been established by the Spirit, and an invitation to join the movement under the messianic lordship of Jesus.

In Christ (as we saw in chapter 5), we are called to a relationship that transcends national loyalties, language barriers, sexual difference, racial distinctions, religious suspicion, social class, and economic rivalry (Gal. 3:27-28; Col. 3:10-11). The Christ "who is our peace" has "brought us together" in a way no political figure could ever do. He has demolished the barriers to peace. For those "resurrected with Christ," the old mores and etiquette, status symbols, religious and cultural taboos, national ideologies, and standards of living no longer determine the structure of community relationship.

It is important to note that these categories of change "in Christ" are social, legal, political, and economic. They have to do with more than attitudes and intentions of the heart. They speak to the structure and character of the human community under the rule of God. They are not simply spiritual or religious ideals which we have no mandate to implement in the social order. The "in Christ" position is not a haven of mystical satisfaction and tranquillity but a new moral and social possibility in the community of God's peace.[5]

Far too long the more orthodox Protestant religious tradition in countries like the United States and South Africa has been content to preach a gospel of spiritual peace which does not fundamentally affect the social structure. According to this gospel, lily-white congregations could enjoy "spiritual" kinship and peace with black Christians who would be unwelcome to the fellowship in person.

Preachers and lay people alike could join in the political game of denouncing street violence in the name of peace while doing nothing to alleviate the unjust, frustrating conditions which sparked the violence. Popular evangelists living in relative luxury could spend millions of dollars to preach spiritual peace with God to people caught in the impossible and soul-destroying trap of poverty and disease without lifting a finger to help.

According to this "gospel," military personnel could wreak indiscriminate death and destruction in their bombing in Vietnam with the peace of God in their hearts. Without challenging the military policy, a nationally honored evangelist could stand by the president and pray for him personally as he announced such destruction on Iraq in the name of peace. Indeed, to raise the issue of militarism in the name of evangelical witness earns one the labels of peripheral, disruptive, unpatriotic, and naive—and the labels are hurled not only by the political community but also by fellow evangelical Christians. There seems to have been a blackout in the "city set on a hill" (Matt. 5:14).

The message of peace, therefore, comes first to the church, calling it again to be the prophetic community which demonstrates the peace of God in the midst of selfish competition and violence. As the community of the Spirit, it is exhorted to bear the fruit of the Spirit, which is "love, joy, peace, patience, kindness, generosity, faithfulness, gentleness, and self-control" (Gal. 5:22, NRSV).

The essential character of this community of peace is found in the new *koinonia* that was initiated at Pentecost. Under the impulse of the Spirit, the first congregation at Jerusalem instinctively moved to fulfill the highest precept of commonality found in the law of Moses, that is, the "year of Jubilee" (see Deut. 14:28—15:11 and Lev. 25).

According to that law, the earth and its wealth belong to God. Therefore wealth was to be distributed according to the needs of God's people. The land was not to be sold "in perpetuity" (Lev. 25:23). To make allowance for human failures, periodic redistributions were to be made, culminating every fifty years in the "year of the Lord's release." At that time debts were to be canceled, family properties lost by misfortune were to be returned, and in general the poor were to have a chance to even the score and begin anew.

This law was never fully obeyed under the old covenant. Gradually the imbalance of poverty and wealth increased. Conditions that led finally to Israel's collapse and captivity developed. The Jubilee idea as a time of God's favor came to be associated with the messianic rule, as we see in Isaiah 61:2 and in the Magnificat (Luke 1:51-53).

Jesus himself recognized and underscored the validity of Isaiah's prophecy when he quoted it in the synagogue at Nazareth to describe his own mission (Luke 4:18-19). He said that he had come to proclaim release and "the year of the Lord's favor" (NRSV). So the community that confessed Jesus to be the Messiah on the day of Pentecost immediately moved in the spirit of Jubilee to distribute their wealth according to the needs of all concerned. Thus they sought again to reestablish the peace of God in anticipation of the messianic reign.

While this instinctive expression does not provide a literal blueprint for organizing the church, it clearly enunciates the fundamental spirit and form of the new community of peace. Two opposing principles of organization are explicitly named. The one is *koinos* or commonality. The other is *idios* or individualism. We are told that no one said of his possessions, "They are *idios*"; they held their possessions *koinos* (Acts 4:32). Two spirits are strikingly portrayed. Koinos is a spirit of openness and sharing—not in the sense of "charity" but as an act of fair play and justice. Idios is a spirit of privacy and self-interest.

This first Christian congregation organized its life on the principle of commonality of interest and the conviction that the individual self can find realization and fulfillment only in the shared experience of the reconciled community. This is in striking contrast to the social contract theory on which our democratic society today is based. The contract is assumed to be between private competitive egos; it is based on the principle of enlightened self-interest and a balance of power.[6] These are two different and conflicting concepts of peace; and the one based on koinonia is the essence of the New Testament.

The Anabaptists of the sixteenth century who sought to take this vision of the New Testament church seriously were called perfectionists and "heaven stormers." They were considered ones who tried to get to heaven by good works. Today "naive" and "socialist" seem more effective epithets. In light of this, we must stress that no single economic or political plan is being suggested as a blueprint of the kingdom. No definitive pattern has been or will be humanly devised to perfectly organize the peace of God. No legalized formulas can or will ever fully express the Spirit of koinonia.

What is seriously amiss in the life of American evangelicalism, however, is its defection from the koinonia principle and its identification of private property (idios) and enlightened self-interest with the New Testament ideal. Starting from this assumption, evangelicalism has failed through the years to take seriously the mission of peace and justice which Jesus himself proclaimed and committed to the church.

Nor is this koinonia principle applicable only to individuals in the church community. The peace of God proclaimed by Christ and his apostles is not a purely individual matter. Those in public office also stand under the law of the God who disclosed himself in Christ. The faithful church also must direct its message of peace to the "principalities and powers," to those in positions of public authority and responsibility.

In the final *epiphany* (manifestation) Christ will be revealed as "Lord of lords"—ruler over those exercising public authority. Under the rule of Christ the peace of God will not be imposed by arbitrary might, but by intrinsic right. The "rod of iron" is not a rod of despotic, arbitrary power! *And this intrinsic right even now lays claims upon governments and all public powers.* Even though "the kingdom of God and his righteousness" are not yet fully vindicated, the church proclaims its conviction that kingdom principles are even now the ultimate standard of justice and peace.

The easy assumption of two ethical standards—one for believers' private lives and one for public policy and action—has played havoc with the church's witness to the lordship of Christ. It has led to accommodation and support of the political status quo, with the plea that nothing more can be expected of the secular state. It has allowed Christians in control of business and industry to justify admittedly sub-Christian standards of operation in their company activity while carefully maintaining a high personal morality.

Even more serious, in a kind of reflexive thrust it has led to accommodations with worldliness in the church itself. Fellow members of Christ deal with each other according to the patterns and norms set for secular social institutions. The democratic process has become the formula for peace. Even in the church it is each person for her or himself. Koinonia has been transformed into camaraderie and "auld acquaintance."

The message of peace must be a word spoken by a faithful church to remind the government and other centers of power that their authority is not their own but God's. Therefore their exercise of power stands under the judgment of Christ, the final revelation of God. That is true now, not only in the age to come.

Finally, the gospel of peace calls the church to *peacemaking*. The God Movement is a shalom movement, and a peacemaker is one who works for the movement. (I have used *shalom* for peace in this case because the word peace, like love, has become vulgarized, and to make the point here some precision of meaning is required.)

We have generally assumed that when Jesus said, "Blessed are the peacemakers," he meant the trucemakers, arbitrators, conciliators, and pacifiers. Certainly in its broader sense it may include all who work for just and peaceable solutions to human conflict. But more precisely a "peacemaker" is one who works in and for the God Movement to bring about shalom, which includes peace with God and human beings.

The hallmark of Christian peacemaking is the ministry of reconciling people to God (2 Cor. 5:20-21). As we have seen in chapter 5, this means initially bringing them into the revolutionary community of peace under the lordship of Christ. For the mission of peacemaking we must have volunteers who have first made peace with God and themselves. Nothing less than a radical conversion from *idios* to *koinonia* will do. They must, as Jesus said, "be born of the Spirit."

This Holy Spirit of koinonia is the spirit of agape that casts out the fear and insecurity which cause humans to clutch their possessions. It is the spirit of gratitude that in Christ all things belong to us, so we are freed from competition and possessiveness. It is the spirit of

contentment and reconciliation to life or death because Jesus Christ is Lord of both.

And perhaps we should also be explicit about what
it is not. It is not the spirit of *asceticism*, which rejects
the goodness of material things to achieve perfection.
Neither is it the spirit of an extreme *mysticism*, which
sometimes denigrate the goods of this life as opposed
to the spiritual. Nor is it the spirit of secularistic *communism*, which demeans individual worth in the name
of group values and goals. Spiritual birth introduces a
genuinely new revolutionary quality into life.

Only when we begin to understand the radicalness
of Christian peacemaking can we understand the absolute necessity for radical conversion. The mission of
peace is a "mission impossible." It confronts the
worldly establishment with the offensive announcement that through Christ God has shown its wisdom
to be foolishness (*moronic* in the Greek) and its power
to be weakness. And it follows this pronouncement
with the politically naive call to find peace through the
way of the cross. (See 1 Cor. 1:18-25.)

Christian peacemakers operate on three principal
convictions which are disclosed throughout the prophetic tradition of both the Old and New Testaments.
The first is that the world and all that is in it belongs to
God. This revealed axiom stands in direct contrast to
the human assumption that the wealth of this world is
the private property of individuals who have a right to
use it for self-aggrandizement.

The second conviction is that all human beings share
equally in God's loving concern. This contrasts with
the tribal assumption that in his inscrutable provi-

dence God has shown favoritism to some people.[7]

The third conviction is that koinonia is the formula for peace. Because we share God's love equally, sharing God's wealth is a principle of justice. This stands in sharp contrast to the formula for peace assumed in power politics—namely, that justice is based on the political balance of competitive self-interest.

Based on these principles, the ministry of peacemaking inevitably leads to identification with the poor and oppressed. Peacemakers heal the sick and wounded, free the slaves and those unjustly imprisoned, feed the hungry, and care for the rejected and alienated. They work for the vindication of God's kingdom and his justice.[8] Peacemakers are those who "hunger and thirst to see right prevail" (Matt. 5:6, NEB).

In light of this, it is obvious that men and women who have caught the new vision of God's rule of peace can never again be uncritically loyal to their old homeland. They are now citizens of a new "holy nation," under a new authority and working from different presuppositions (1 Pet. 2:9-10). To simply conform to the pattern of this age (Rom. 12:1-2) is an act of disloyalty against the new government to which they have pledged allegiance. Status-seeking, selfish competition and accumulation of wealth, violence, discrimination, injustice, impiety, and the like are simply intolerable to the renewed mind.

In Western cultures, including the United States, Christianity has tended to play a supportive and complementary role to civil religion. While religion was politically disestablished in the United States, Protestantism, the predominant religion, continued to be a kind of "social establishment." Thus it tended to identify with the public social ethic and confine its religious morality to the individual. In such a climate the evangelical churches became so identified with the national ego that they failed to see the radical implication of nonconformity at the systemic level.

Sectarian Christianity has also failed to apply Romans 12:1 to the systemic level, but for other reasons. It has emphasized "separation from the world," and has applied the biblical ethic to individuals within the church. The ethical principle of nonconformity has been applied almost entirely to "personal" matters such as use of alcoholic beverages, illicit sexual behavior, attendance at "worldly amusements."

Of course the principle of nonconformity applies to individual behavioral patterns. With the serious disintegration of traditional morals in the past decades, we have become increasingly aware of the serious impact individual behavior can have on the moral and physical health of society. But the appalling violence, crime, injustice, and disease in our world is due to more than the cumulative effect of individual misbehavior. It is systemic. That is, it is actually built into our social, political, and economic systems. Ironically it took a Hindu reading the Christian New Testament to reintroduce the importance of "nonconformity to this world" at the systemic level.[9]

Peacemakers will always need to confront the secular system with noncooperation because that system is essentially based on the principle of competitive self-interest. There seems to be confusion about this among many Christians today. In many minds the political freedom of the democratic system has been virtually equated with freedom in Christ.[10] The peace legally imposed by a majority has been equated with the peace of God, and the democratic process has been identified with justice. On the basis of these assumptions, it is simply taken for granted that the *Christian* way to work for peace and justice is to work through the political system for orderly change.

While we greatly appreciate the democratic system, and can on many occasions work through the political process, we must also keep clearly in mind that secular democracy is based on the *self-interest of the majority*. It is not rooted in justice as such. It is to be hoped that this majority will be enlightened with a sense of justice, but Christians should never confuse the "justice" of the majority written into statutory law with the justice of God's kingdom. Peacemakers live not by majority opinion but by the new law of Christ. Their lifestyle reflects the way of peace. Their nonconformed presence in the world as strangers should confront and sensitize the public conscience.

The God Movement introduced a revolution into human affairs, and revolutions are never quiet affairs without stress and strain. Jesus himself said, "I am come to cast fire upon the earth. . . ." And again he said, "I did not come to bring peace but a sword." Paul and Silas were described as men who turned the world upside down. In an evil world peace can never mean the quiet of withdrawal or accommodation. The Movement aggressively promotes the peace of God as central to its evangelical message and task.

It seems appropriate to end this chapter as we began

it, with words from Menno Simons' tract on *The New Birth*.

> This regeneration of which we write, from which comes the penitent, pious life that has the promise, can only originate in the Word of the Lord, rightly taught and rightly understood and received in the heart by faith through the Holy Ghost. . . .
>
> These regenerated people have a spiritual king over them who rules them by the unbroken scepter of His mouth, namely, with His Holy Spirit and Word. . . . His name is Christ Jesus.
>
> They are the children of peace who have beaten their swords into plowshares and their spears into pruning hooks, and know war no more. They give to Caesar the things that are Caesar's and to God the things that are God's.
>
> Their sword is the sword of the Spirit, which they wield in a good conscience through the Holy Ghost. . . .
>
> Their kingdom is a kingdom of grace, here in hope and after this in eternal life. . . .
>
> Their citizenship is in heaven, and they use the lower creations with thanksgiving and to the necessary support of their own lives, and to the free service of their neighbor, according to the Word of God (Wenger, 1956:93-94).

7

The Spirit of Love

If peace is the message and mission of the community of the Spirit, its inner quality and dynamic is *agape* love. In the last chapter we examined the concept of peace as a right pattern of relationships with God and our fellows. Now we must look carefully at the love that motivates and guides the community in its quest for peace. "God's love has been poured into our hearts through the Holy Spirit" (Rom. 5:5, NRSV) is the truly revolutionary characteristic of the God Movement.

We have, in fact, reached a crucial point in our examination of the God Movement. We have seen that the "peace of God" calls for a radical change in human relationships, and that the followers of Christ are to aggressively promote this radical change. Like Paul and Silas of old, they should be turning the world upside down. Is this simply another idealistic appeal to violence for the sake of establishing peace? If it is not—and it is not—then the secret must lie in this spirit of agape which informs both the character and method of the peace revolution.

Karl Marx, the father of modern communism, is quoted as having said, "My goal is to change the world." At his best Marx was interested in justice and equity in the social order. In some respects he reminds one of the Hebrew prophets who cried out in anger against the rich oppressors. But Marx's method for bringing about such a revolution was force and violence. He was convinced that the wealthy bourgeoisie would never give up their privilege by choice. Therefore he taught that they must be overcome by violent revolution.

As we are well aware, this basic Marxist assumption led modern communism to justify violence, intrigue, exploitation, and oppression as legitimate means to bring about a revolution of peace and justice. Finally after some seven decades of coercion and violence we have seen the demise of that socialistic vision.

Jesus too was interested in a revolution of peace and justice. But in diametrical contrast to Marx, Jesus taught that the only method which can bring about true peace and justice is love.

In the story of Jesus' temptations (Matt. 4:1-11), we are told that Satan offered him three popular ways to be a successful revolutionary leader. First, he urged Jesus to use miraculous power to make bread and feed the people. The suggestion was that if Jesus could promise the hungry multitudes food, he could command their allegiance. He might become a benevolent dictator.

In the second temptation, Satan told Jesus to become a great religious leader and miracle worker. Through the display of supernatural power he could impress the crowds and become a great authoritative leader.

When Jesus rejected this suggestion, Satan made his last appeal. He showed Jesus all the "kingdoms of the world." Then Satan offered to give the world to Jesus if he would fall at Satan's feet and worship. This was the temptation to build an empire rooted in the use of force and "worldly" power. Satan suggested that Jesus could gain power as the Caesars had—through war and violence. As they had imposed the "peace of Rome" on the ancient Near Eastern world, so Jesus could at last impose the true peace of God.

Jesus rejected all three demonic substitutes for the way of the cross. His revolution was to be radically new. It was to be the revolution of *agape*.

Eros, Philia, and Agape

The whole of the Mosaic Law is summed up in the word *love*, Paul wrote to the Christians at Rome (Rom. 13:10). Jesus also said that love of God and neighbor is the greatest commandment and encompasses the whole intention of the Law (Matt. 22:37-40). However, because the English word love has so many possible meanings, it has become ambiguous. We must find a more specific term to carry its meaning in this context.

What kind of love fulfills the law? What kind of "new commandment" has Jesus left for his disciples? The Greek language contains three words which can be translated love. They are *eros, philia,* and *agape*. Each word has its own distinct meaning, and the writers of the New Testament use one almost exclusively. It is the word *agape*.

First there is the word *eros*, which means desire. The moral quality of eros is determined by the nature of the object desired. When the object is good, then eros is virtuous. When the object is illicit, eros is lust. Eros itself is neither good nor bad. It is essentially a passion or impulse aroused by an object which seems desirable. It is a strong motivator toward action which will satisfy the craving—whether for God, knowledge, or some less worthy object.[1]

Eros is the dynamic of all social relationships based upon self-interest. Advertisers, politicians, and educators all attempt in one way or another to manipulate or condition desire to achieve their goals. Political philosophers have argued that in the long run the greatest good for the largest number is also good for each individual; therefore we ought to desire the good of the majority.

National leaders attempt to persuade citizens that altruistic aid to less fortunate countries is in their own best interests and often explicitly promise the government will do only what is in the national self-interest. Advertisers try to persuade the public that one brand of bandages, cold medicine, or breakfast cereals is more desirable. Educators contend that knowledge is the means to the highest human end. Society is rooted in self-interest and motivated by eros.

The second word for love in the Greek language is *philia*, which denotes the mutual or reciprocal relations of friendship. This is the love of camaraderie and mutual trust. It is, as Aristotle long ago pointed out, the very basis of political community and even family solidarity. Cooperatives and mutual insurance societies are good examples of such reciprocal helpfulness in the world of economics. The United Nations is an extension of philia, from the local and national levels to world relationships.

Philia is really a variety of eros. It is enlightened self-interest based on prudent trust. Trust is the new element but it is conditioned by trustworthiness and mutuality. Both of these prudential elements are important to philia. A friend must gain our confidence—we must have reason to believe him or her worthy of confidence. But the benefits of friendship must go both ways. There is an intrinsic element of pragmatism in philia. Whether consciously or not, philia calculates the advantages of friendship for itself.

Eros and philia were the words most commonly used in classical and Hellenistic Greek. However, eros is never used in the New Testament, and philia is not prominent. Perhaps it was precisely because the word *agape* was so nondescript and unused that the early Christians made it their word.[2] That way they could fill it with their own newly found meaning. While agape has a broad usage, essentially it describes the quality of love disclosed in Jesus Christ. As John says, "We know love [agape] by this, that he [Christ] laid down his life for us" (1 John 3:16, NRSV).

Agape has a unique quality that goes beyond both eros and philia. It is not a response to the desirable, lovable, or admirable but to the needy—the undesired and unloved. Its essence is revealed not in response to a friend but to an enemy. Agape seeks to create a loving response in the unloving. It initiates action when prudent self-interest does not necessarily dictate such action. Agape acts unilaterally! It accepts the burden of vulnerability because it respects the other person and always hopes for the best (1 Cor. 13:7). That is why the supreme symbol of agape is the cross.

Such action is not only difficult in the doing; it is difficult in the conception! So difficult that what we have done in the name of Christian agape has in fact been a subtle self-serving charity. Whether our concepts have shaped our actions or merely described them after the fact, the church has by and large reduced agape to charity or benevolence.

At least since the days of Charles G. Finney and the "benevolent empire" built on the evangelical revivals of the 1830s, evangelicalism has accepted charitable altruism or benevolence as the working definition for agape.[3] In effect we have based our life in the community of the Spirit on the principle of philia. We have then urged sacrificial altruism as a counsel of perfection. But—and we must say it emphatically—agape is *not* benevolence! Its goal is not "charity," which implies superior virtue on the part of the giver. Its goal is rather fairness, which implies humility and a genuine identification with the needy.

In his critique of the new morality, the late Bishop Pike called attention to the definition of agape as benevolence and rejected it as an adequate basis for Christian ethics. He pointed out that when we "love the unlovely and unlovable" we are implicitly and inescapably belittling the beloved object. "For it [agape—benevolence] to be recognizably operative it is intrinsically requisite that the other be assessed as unlovable, unworthy, undeserving, *no good* (Cox, 1968:199; emphasis added)."

Pike's criticism was aimed directly at Joseph Fletcher's "situation ethic" based on love, but it applies equally to all systems that equate agape and benevolence. It is important to note the precise use of words like "unlovely," "unlovable," or "unlikable" as the object of agape. That is quite different from making its object the "unloved" and "undesired." When benevolence makes the former its object, Pike notes, "It supplies a sense of goodness and well-doing to one person while *belittling* the other" (Cox, 1968:198-199; emphasis added). In this insight, Pike has exposed the worm in the apple of much Christian charity.

In the teaching of Jesus, the object of agape is not the unworthy person but the enemy. Enemy, like friend, describes how I view the other person. It is a projection of my feelings of fear and vulnerability onto that person. If there are also feelings of unworthiness, they are just that—my feelings projected onto the object. Fear turns an opponent, real or imagined, into an enemy. Agape transcends fear and hostility, enabling the one who loves to see and respect the worth of an enemy. As John puts it with beautiful simplicity, "Perfect love [agape] casts out fear" (1 John 4:18).

While there are intimations of agape in creation and glimpses of it in human history, its essential nature became clear only when God revealed the unique and inalienable worth of all humankind in the incarnation. From the Christian perspective, a person's worth does not depend upon education, wealth, sex, nationality, race, or ideological convictions. As Paul wrote in 2 Corinthians 5:16, "With us therefore worldly standards have ceased to count in our estimate of any man" (NEB).

Agape takes self and self-interest out of the center as prime measure of worth.[4] It recognizes the worth of all persons as creatures beloved and esteemed of God in spite of any real or imagined threat persons might pose to us. Agape is not a response of charity to the unworthy. It is a reaching out with good will to the enemy and friend alike. It is like God's love, which indiscriminately sends rain and sunshine on the just and unjust (Matt. 5:45-46).

Agape implies selflessness in the sense of not being selfish. It does not, however, imply self-rejection. It no more requires the "belittling" of oneself than of the other! Only those who know God and stand confident of their own worth in his love are strong to love as he loves. This was the beauty and strength of Jesus himself. Fully aware "that he had come from God and was going back to God," he became the servant whose service dignified and enhanced the lives of those whom he served (John 13:3-4). And he called his disciples to follow his example in such agapeic service (vv. 15-17).

It may be obvious by this time that love leads to action. Love is a verb before it becomes a noun. Agape love is love as expressed in koinonia action. We are not to love in theory and talk but in deed and truth, wrote John. And he pressed his point with the rhetorical question, "How does God's love abide in anyone who has the world's goods and sees a brother or sister in need and yet refuses help?" (1 John 3:17-18, NRSV).

Love as Identification

Agape is redemptive involvement in the sin and suffering of the world. We have come to know agape in God's incarnation, in his becoming a human among humankind, sharing our lot, making himself a servant, and bearing our hostility and sin to create a response of love in us. In this same way, through our expression of God's love in action, the world comes to know God's love. Again John clearly suggests that we now stand in the same relation to God and under the same mandate to make his love known (John 17:18; 1 John 4:12).

Richard Keithahn, a longtime missionary to India, told how a noncaste peasant once threw himself at Keithahn's feet in a posture of worship. Keithahn and his wife lived with the people in the village and ministered as best they could to their needs. The peasant's action was intended as an expression of gratitude for the genuine concern the Keithahns had shown him. Keithahn, however, was embarrassed and a bit irritated that one man should pay such worshipful respect to another.

He pulled the man to his feet saying, "Get up. I am not God."

Not to be rebuffed, the peasant replied, "Yes, Sahib, but we never saw God until you came."

God's agape had been expressed through his servant and had found its mark.

But we must say more. Agape is involvement of a distinct kind. There is a definitive quality or character which distinguishes agape and has implications for the way in which the church is involved in the life of the world.

Agape seeks involvement through *identification* with those it seeks to serve. Jesus himself identified with "the poor." In contrast to the Pharisees, who said, "This multitude is accursed because it knows not the law," Jesus had compassion upon the crowds because they were "as sheep without a shepherd."

Many examples illustrate Jesus' ability to identify with persons to whom he related. He ate with publicans and sinners. He conversed with women—a taboo for rabbis—even with a Samaritan woman and with prostitutes. He earned the reputation of a "drunkard" because of his close association with the lower classes in their festivities. He made the cause of the poor his own and offered them first place in the God Movement (Luke 6:20).

This does not mean Jesus rejected or despised the rich. Neither does it mean he sanctioned uncritically the motives, purposes, and goals of the masses. Indeed, it is clear that he did not. But it does mean Jesus took the side of the oppressed against systemic oppression. Both the poor and the affluent ruling class recognized this. To the rulers his identification with the poor was a threat. To the poor themselves it was their ground of hope.

In order to understand the significance of agapeic identification, we must contrast it to the paternalistic altruism against which Jesus warned his disciples. "The kings of the Gentiles lord it over them; and those in authority over them are called benefactors. But not so with you; rather the greatest among you must become like the youngest, and the leader like one who serves" (Luke 22:25-26, NRSV).

Paternalistic aid is inherently condescending. It assaults the self-respect of the person it attempts to help. It demands, whether covertly or openly, that the recipient recognize the benefactor's right to superior status and power, and therefore his right to control the use of what he has donated. At the same time, it expects recognition of the donor's goodness and therefore gratitude properly expressed in submission and humility.

Such an assumed right is entirely foreign to agape. The example of Jesus as described by Paul in Philippians 2:5-8 is the model for agapeic action. He laid aside his "God form" and took the "servant form." This was the essence of his "emptying" himself. He presented himself as a man without status or power. To do this, he completely assumed human "likeness," taking on himself our existential handicap, struggling with our temptations and suffering our death. He was born a Galilean among Jews, a peasant among peasants. He could not pull rank because he had no rank to pull. Such is the identification of agape.

The words of Jesus against paternalism were never more appropriate for the Christian church. Following from its understanding of agape as benevolence, the church has, with the best intentions, identified with the affluent and served the poor from a position of paternal strength. It has ministered *to* the poor but has seldom been the voice of the poor. It has run programs *for* the poor to improve their conditions and status. The church has then defined such improvement in its own terms and often in its own self-interest.

Even in programs of evangelism, the church has not acted as one "beggar telling another beggar where to find bread" but as a rich patron lifting beggars out of misfortune. Evangelistic strategies have been taken from advertising and marketing and depend on multimillions of dollars for high tech propaganda. Thus a wealthy church justifies its riches as a special blessing from God for its benevolent witness.

Identification implies respect for the dignity of other people and understanding of their situation and feelings. At its best this is the agapeic meaning of mutuality in love. In contrast to philia, mutuality rooted in agape calls for koinonia, for fraternal relationship and responsibility which rests not on mutual ability to reciprocate but on an agapeic identification with others in need which makes them neighbors.

Jesus illustrated this dimension of agape mutuality in the story of the good Samaritan (Luke 10:25-37). When Jesus said that the first and second commandments were to love God and "your neighbor as yourself," a lawyer asked, "Who is my neighbor?" Who am I mutually responsible to love as myself? On the basis of philia, that seemed a perfectly proper question.

The lawyer was, of course, aware of the canons of mutuality and friendship. According to the standards of philia a neighbor would be defined as one who reciprocates in mutual ties of friendship and responsibility. Such ties are formed by familial, religious, or national relationships—Romans to Romans, Galileans to Galileans, Jews to Jews.

But in the stark clarity of the parable, Jesus said that agape makes everyone in need a neighbor. Agape obligates me, not as a paternalistic benefactor to an act of altruism, but as a brother or sister for whom a mutual debt of assistance is obligatory without further ado.

Certainly this is the way we should understand Jesus' words when he said, "Give to him who begs from you, and do not refuse him who would borrow from you" (Matt. 5:42). He was not encouraging impetuous, irresponsible charity, which can be as demeaning of persons as paternalism. Rather, he was recommending a generous spirit which recognizes a "neighbor" in everyone who has need and which accepts agape responsibility for him or her.

In obligations of agape mutuality, no questions are asked about the ability of the recipient to reciprocate. It is enough to have been privileged to befriend a neighbor. Those who "gave a cup of cold water" in the name of Christ were not conscious they had done anything deserving of reward (Matt. 25:37). The service of agape is an end in itself because it fulfills the very meaning of humanity both in the giver and receiver. It is its own intrinsic reward.

Agape identification applies even to enemies. It assumes the burden of their misunderstanding and hostility. Undoubtedly the unfortunate Jew on the road to Jericho would have despised and rejected his benefactor in other circumstances. ("For Jews have no dealings with Samaritans," John 4:9). But the Samaritan did not bother to inquire into the Jew's attitudes or to use them as an excuse. Agape bears the burden of proof in such a case. It seeks out need even in the face of antipathy and rejection and finds a way to serve as neighbor.

Agapeic Justice

On first thought it may seem strange to speak of a loving justice. In the Western Christian tradition, love and justice have been contrasted and love has been associated with mercy and grace. When justice is identified with morally equivalent punishment—"an eye for an eye, and a tooth for a tooth," love as mercy pleads for forgiveness. When justice is considered as a standard for distribution of goods, it is generally defined as a minimum one might rightly expect. Love then is conceived as grace which goes beyond the minimum and gives more than is deserved. This is the "plus" of benevolence or charity.

As we have noted earlier, the theological rationale of Protestantism has been heavily influenced by these concepts and definitions. Sin is a transgression which incurs moral guilt. Justice is the equivalent penalty which matches the quantity of guilt incurred. Love as mercy and grace is then disclosed in Christ who paid the just penalty for the offense. Indeed, following Luther some theologies have called Christ "the Greatest Criminal," meaning the one who pays the penalty of all criminals.

The language of penalty, just retribution, and mercy does not logically require associating guiltiness with worthlessness. But historically in orthodoxy the concept of moral guilt has in fact subtly come to imply lack of moral value. The notion of personal offense has been translated into the language of moral debauchery and unworthiness. Agape has thus been understood as God's response to the unworthy—the nobody and the no-good.

Accordingly, justice provided for behavior toward persons based on their actual worth (the merits of the case). Meanwhile love, defined as grace, dispensed with the category of worth or merit on the assumption that the recipient was actually unworthy. In either case worth was calculated according to the rules of philia—worth to society, or worth to me. The great human temptation is to reduce all relationships to the level of philia, where they can be dealt with in political and psychological business as usual.

The idea that human beings as sinners have less worth stems from Augustine and his Platonic assumptions. Implicit in his concept of "original sin" and the fall of humanity is the loss of some key element of humanity itself and thus of value. When the change resulting from the fall is seen as changing actual human nature, it is almost impossible to avoid a negative valuation of the sinner as a defective person—or so it has proved in the history of Christian theology.

This is a fine but important point, because it marks a watershed between a Christianity that accommodates itself to the old politics of philia and eros, and the new community of agape. Offense against goodness is real and has moral consequences. Offense causes pain and hostility. It destroys personal relationships and personal character. For these reasons the offender may properly be called offensive and guilty. And such offense must be taken care of if the damage to relationships is to be repaired.

But here is the crux. By the standards of eros, offenders are not only unloved and undesired, but also undesirable and unlovely. By the canons of philia, offenders are unworthy of friendship. But divine agape, while acknowledging the full weight of the offense, turns a different direction. Agape persists in recognizing the offender's dignity and the worthwhileness of reconciliation. *This recognition of the worth and right of the offender is the agapeic basis of justice.* God has indeed taken sin very seriously!

Deserving of forgiveness? Does that not contradict the very concept of God's grace? Not necessarily; it only enlarges it to include God's creative as well as redemptive activity under the category of grace. In the incarnation of "the Word," God revealed that creation itself is an act of agape. Therefore grace is not simply a redemptive response to things gone wrong. *Agape is grace bestowing worth in the very act of creating a person.*

If this were a volume of systematic theology, we might enlarge on the theological implications of this view.[5] Here we only note its implication for the mission of the church. When the community of God's Spirit makes agape the formative principle, its ministry of reconciliation will be motivated and informed by a spirit of moral justice rather than charitable altruism.

The message of agape is that God does not view the human situation in terms of philia—not even in its most exalted moral sense where friendship goes out of its way to show benevolence and grace. There is no condescension in agape! From the divine point of view, perishing humankind is worth saving. Restoring the relationship broken by sin is worth the painful reconciliation. Precisely that is the revelation of love in Jesus Christ.

Agape introduces us to a world of relationships in which forgiveness is a matter of justice. John says, "[God] is faithful and *just*, and will forgive our sins" (1 John 1:9; emphasis added). In the world of agape, even "if the same person sins against you seven times a day, and turns back to you seven times and says, 'I repent,' you must forgive" (Luke 17:4, NRSV). In the agape world "just deserts" are not tallied up like wages for hours worked—"So the last will be first, and the first last" (Matt. 20:1-16).

Under the new law of agape, one is morally bound to "go the second mile" and to "turn the other cheek." The highest measure of justice in the God Movement is expressed in vindicating the helpless and showing compassion to the poor. In one word, agapeic justice is *koinonia*.

It is important to realize that agape is not simply a "counsel of perfection" for individuals to emulate. Rather, it is the spirit and essence of life in the community of the Spirit. Agape is the standard requirement of the law of Christ. Obedience to his new law gives no one special status. Neither is it an unrealistic ideal, or "impossible possibility," as Reinhold Niebuhr has called it, which always judges and forgives our inevitably imperfect attempts to reach it.

Agapeic justice is the "new righteousness" which provides the organizing principle for the community (Matt. 5:20; Rom. 12:9-21; 13:8). It is the moral basis for the new politics of love. We do not perfectly fulfill it, but that is not because it is an impossible principle which can only be approximated in a lower standard of natural justice. Those "who walk not according to the flesh but according to the Spirit," Paul writes, can fulfill "the just requirement of the law." This is precisely what God accomplished by "sending his own Son in the likeness of sinful flesh" (Rom. 8:3-4).

To speak of agape as a spirit and attitude does not answer the hard questions of how such a koinonia is to be organized. Indeed, given the limited and conditional nature of human cultures, there is probably no one universal blueprint for an agapeic social organization. A means of dealing with failure will be a fundamental need. Thus repentance and forgiveness must be at the working center of the community of the Spirit.

What has been attempted here is the more modest task of writing a prologue to the politics of agape. By the same token, what has been criticized is not the human failure of the church to perfect an agapeic system. What deserves criticism is the church's failure to recognize the radically new character of agape and to acknowledge that it is indeed the standard for organizing the life and mission of the church.

The church as one of the institutional "orders of creation," to use Luther's concept, has assumed that the order of natural justice tempered by love is the formative principle of its life. Thus it operates according to the assumptions of Western capitalistic society without serious critique. For example, the church has assumed that the "sacred right of private property" justifies the accumulation of excessive wealth when earned in accordance with the economic and legal canons of the system. For all practical purposes, then, Christian stewardship has been defined as giving a tithe. Charity has been conceived as spontaneous altruism and "sacrifice" rather than the obligation of justice.

In the area of criminal justice, the church has by the same token justified and supported the state's definition of "just penalty" for crime, even to the extent of capital punishment. It has sanctified legalized vengeance as a right of the victimized, and at most has asked that justice be tempered with mercy. Until recently the concepts of victim offender reconciliation, prisoner's rights, and incarceration as correction and rehabilitation have come largely from the secular disciplines of social work and social psychology. Even now, the weight of evangelical opinion supports concepts of criminal justice based on the rational and political structures of philia and eros.

In the same way both Roman Catholic and Protestant orthodoxy has supported the validity of war. It only asks that the war be "just." And the definition of justified violence has largely ruled out the violence of those who are exploited against systems which rule and exploit them. Justice has usually been biased in favor of the established order, which often includes the church.

But the "heretical" definitions and assumptions of philia have been most devastating in the missionary crusade of the church to Christianize and civilize the "heathen."[6] The missionaries fully expected their converts to adopt the patterns of a "higher" civilization. The argument between those who espoused evangelization rather than Christianization concerned only the methods of approach. The very word "heathenism" denoted inferiority, and the sacrifice of the missionaries was described openly in the language of condescension to inferiors. Funds to run the enterprise were collected as charities for which the home churches expected gratitude as well as conformity to their wishes.

The mission was often imposed on the basis of imperialistic violence which was implicit if not explicit. It is common knowledge that the great Western missionary advance of the eighteenth and nineteenth centuries was based on the imperialistic expansion of Western nations. From many a pulpit, liberal as well as fundamentalist, it was avowed that the guns of victorious American soldiers opened the way for the gospel. Many evangelical leaders justified wars against communism on the grounds that missionary activity would be curtailed if communists won the struggle. This was more than tacit admission that the missionary enterprise had been based on violence.[7]

This is not a criticism of individual missionaries who gave their lives for the sake of Christ. Most missionaries have been persons of integrity. They have served with genuine compassion and concern. Often the Spirit of love has been genuinely manifest in their ministries, despite the assumptions, organization, and methods of the missionary enterprise.

But the time has come to recognize that the theological and ethical rationale of American Protestantism is inadequate to provide a self-understanding and strategy for the decades ahead. Evangelicalism has enthusiastically endorsed "church growth" without reexamining its guiding theological rationale.

The agapeic mission is motivated by the simple fact of human need and God's love which obligates us to our neighbor. "For the love of Christ urges us on," wrote Paul. "And he died for all, so that those who live might live no longer for themselves . . ." (2 Cor. 5:14-15, NRSV). The incarnation furnishes the model of identification with those to whom agape is directed. Again in the words of Paul, agape becomes "all things to all people." Its service "in the name of Christ" attaches no strings. In short, its purpose is to reconcile humanity to itself and to God, not to spread a Western Christian civilization.

8

The Community's Witness to Grace

In chapter 4 we referred to the church as a "propaganda ministry for the God Movement." Now in this concluding chapter we will explore further the implications for evangelism of what we have learned about the community of the Spirit.

We have noted that the gospel message is that promise has become reality in Christ. That reality is not fully achieved in the church. The salvation so beautifully symbolized in Revelation by the "holy city, new Jerusalem, coming down out of heaven from God" (21:2—22:5; 3:12) remains a hope for the future. However, a new stage has been initiated in which Spirit displaces law as the guide and dynamic of the saving community. Paul succinctly described this reality as "the power of God for salvation" (Rom. 1:16).

We have observed that the reality of salvation as it is presented in the New Testament includes more than the life, death, and resurrection of Jesus. Pentecost and the beginning of the church also belong to the gospel. The new koinonia of the Spirit is the anticipatory fulfillment—the community of reconciliation within which salvation is experienced. It is the community of grace formed under the new covenant which we enter through repentance—through fundamental reorientation of our lives to self and to God. In the New Testament, repentance (metanoia) means renouncing our old self-centered life and adopting the new lifestyle of agape demonstrated by Jesus.

This same community, which exists "by grace through faith," is also the community of witness. We have seen that it has the character of a movement always remaining in and for the world. Jesus described it as a "city set on a hill," whose light beckons and guides the weary, lost traveler to the security and camaraderie of a civilized society.[1] In the city there was safety from the marauders who took advantage of the darkness to rob and kill. In a friendly city foreigners could find protection and hospitality. Thus Jesus used the city as a symbol of the saving community whose light shines in the gathering darkness, inviting the traveler to find salvation.

This uniting of the community of grace and the community of witness implies not only an integral relationship between propaganda and reality but also between the message and the method of evangelization. In the well-known phrase of Marshall McLuhan "the medium is the message!" The koinoniac form and the agapeic spirit are simultaneously both message and medium.

Indeed, the merging of method and message is implicit in the word *witness*. Witnesses are not ones who repeat what has been told to them, or who have learned a technique of communication. Witnesses are those who have experienced (witnessed) the reality being reported as a testimony (witness). The witness of God's love both to oneself and others is the reality of the Spirit of love dwelling in our hearts (Rom. 8:16; 1 John 4:13-21.)

Perhaps the major problem in our contemporary practice of evangelism is the breach between message and method. The wistful words of one student from India doing graduate study in the United States should haunt our consciences. He said, "I could never become a Christian because I respect the teaching of Jesus too much." Our example and method (reality) had invalidated the message for him.

The inconsistency between method and message is most evident at two points. First is the virtual reduction of evangelism to verbal communication. The emphasis on the past ("once for all") reality of Christ's work has focused our attention on doctrine and verbal communication. Evangelism has been practically equated with speaking the word—and with a special mode of speaking at that.

Evangelistic manuals tell how to ask leading questions, find the right Bible verses, memorize the correct succession of spiritual laws, or saturate the community with religious literature. The way of salvation has been reduced to a spiritual formula and faith to belief that the formula works. Those who attempt to go beyond this faith formula with what is called "power evangelism" tend to focus on the miraculous experience. To a large extent we disassociate salvation from the present reality of a caring, sharing, renewing community.

A second inconsistency between method and message is use of manipulative techniques to achieve conversions. The church uncritically follows the lead of the Madison Avenue advertisers in manipulating people by creating desire, then satisfy that manufactured desire. Taking cues from modern advertising, the church too often turns witnessing into a massive persuasion campaign. Technique and image are substituted for relationships and reality.

The same point may be put another way. In an evangelism workshop a speaker said, "Christians who want to witness for Christ should scratch where it itches." That is, the church should meet need where it is felt. One participant responded, "Yes, but suppose it does not itch where you think it ought to." This concerned Christian, like many of his concerned brothers and sisters, perceived evangelism as a means of producing a sense of need (conviction) which his good news could then relieve.

Evangelism is the effective communication of the good news of the Christ who is alive and at work for the salvation of the world. It is crucial that we rediscover a method of gospel witness which itself will enhance and commend this New Testament message.

The Method of Jesus

There is no reason to make a fetish out of Jesus' methods, but his life and ministry do provide an exemplary pattern for the church's mission. Luke's Gospel more than the others seems to make paradigmatic connections between Jesus' ministry and the continuing mission of the church.

There are indications that Luke intended the story of Jesus sending out the seventy evangelists (10:1-12) as a paradigm of the greater mission of the church. While

Luke is not giving us literal mission instructions, he does clearly articulate the essential nature and approach of mission work.

These disciples sent to represent Jesus and prepare the way for the rule of God go like "lambs in the midst of wolves." They are totally dependent on God for their protection. They are to go without provisions—in other words, without independent security and power. They are to go as people of peace. Where not accepted they are to move on (vv. 3-6).

Then in verses 8-9 Luke gives what we might call the incarnational mandate. "Whenever you enter a town and they receive you, eat what is set before you; heal the sick in it and say to them, 'The kingdom of God has come near to you.' " This outlines a holistic approach to witness.

Three imperatives stand out in this mandate. First, Jesus told the disciples to eat what was set before them. Second, he commissioned them to heal the sick. And last, they were to tell the people that God's kingdom was near at hand. If we paraphrase these imperatives into a more formal methodology, we might say this: First, identify with the people. Second, demonstrate the reality of God's power for reconciliation and healing. Third, announce the nearness of God's saving presence.

Even before we look more carefully at this formula, we should pause to notice that it clearly moves from nonverbal to verbal, not vice versa. The movement is from the attitude and bearing of the messenger to saving action, then to verbal announcement. One cannot help noting that the current pattern of most evangelistic missions moves in the opposite direction.

While there is no reason to insist that this literal sequence be followed in every situation, there is good reason to believe the formula represents a sound principle of communication. And the formula is consistent with the message itself.

Certainly the formula summarizes the apostolic pattern. The message of the apostles was winged with power by the demonstration of the new reality of the Spirit at work among the people. These demonstrations were "signs" of the new reality. They stopped the voice of opposition, if not the opposition itself (Acts 4:21-22).[2]

We need not verify this point with exhaustive reference to all New Testament evidence, but two different types of illustrations can be cited. Luke reports that in the Jerusalem church during the weeks that followed Pentecost, "the apostles gave their testimony to the resurrection of the Lord Jesus [with great power]" (4:33). This statement is made in the context of a description of the new koinonia, which demonstrated the power of the Spirit among the apostolic band. The apostles' reports about the resurrection of Christ had convincing power because everyone could see a demonstration of the living body of Christ! The reality authenticated the witness.

The second illustrative passage is 1 Corinthians 2:4-5. There Paul contrasts persuasive speech, eloquence, and wisdom in the preaching of the gospel with "demonstration of the Spirit and of power." Nothing in these early chapters suggests this "demonstration of the Spirit and of power" simply refers to the emotional impact of Paul's words through some inner endowment of the Spirit. Here at Corinth the power of the Spirit was creating a new community of love in the midst of individualism, rivalry, and self-centered religious ecstasy. It was a body in which Christ was recognized as the "source of . . . life . . . wisdom . . . righteousness . . . sanctification and redemption" (1 Cor. 1:30).

According to Luke, Jesus commissioned the evangelists to begin by identifying themselves with those to whom they would communicate. In the world of Jesus and the apostles, eating together indicated a bond of appreciation, respect, and acceptance. One of Jesus' most serious offenses was his intimate association with the poor who were considered "accursed" because they did not know the law (John 7:49). The Jewish leaders complained against Jesus because he ate with sinners—with tax collectors (collaborators with Rome), common artisans and peasants (the unclean), and worse, even with prostitutes and drunkards. Jesus justified himself by saying, "I have not come to call the righteous, but sinners to repentance."

One of the first lessons Jewish Christians needed to learn was that they should eat with Gentiles. Jewish scruples forbade this, but the new order required new respect for persons of all cultures and religions. Early in their evangelistic efforts, Peter learned he must break the taboo which separated Jews and Gentiles (Acts 10:9-17, 48). Even the "barbarians" (Col. 3:11), that class to which Aristotle accorded less than full human status, were to be accorded dignity.

To identify with persons means to accept and affirm

them. This does not necessarily mean always to agree with or condone. While Jesus identified with the masses in their culture of poverty and championed their cause, he frequently reproved them for their selfishness, lack of faith, and obsession with the material dimensions of life.

Acceptance indicates the ability to see past cultural, moral, ideological, and other differences to the worth of the other person. It implies a genuine appreciation for others which is more than tolerance. Affirmation indicates respect for other persons in their own cultural context. Jesus saw in the vacillating Simon a rock; in the quiet Nathaniel "an Israelite in whom there is no guile"; and in the weeping prostitute a woman with a deep capacity for love. He affirmed them for what in their best moments they most wanted to be.

Acceptance of others is perhaps most concretely expressed in the admission of our need of them. Jesus himself exemplified this acceptance of others in his constant dependence on them. To the Samaritan woman's surprise and delight, he asked her for a drink of water. In a striking public act of acceptance, Jesus invited himself to the home of Zacchaeus for dinner. He constantly relied on his friends, using their boats and homes, eating their food, enjoying their companionship. He needed them! This was the authenticating mark of his real incarnation.

The authentic witness to grace must give up self-sufficiency and independence. That is the inner meaning of Jesus' command to go without provisions and accept the hospitality of the people to whom we would witness. Far too much of our modern witness, both at home and abroad, has assumed the superiority of our cultural stance. We have gone out from a secure economic base which allowed the evangelist independence and distance. Such autonomy in method contradicts the message of incarnation.

We need not belabor the point that evangelists must demonstrate the reality they preach. Jesus himself spent much time and energy healing diseases, feeding the hungry, exorcising demons, and forgiving sinners. In the words of Cleopas, he was indeed "a prophet mighty in deed and word before God and all the people" (Luke 24:19b). Jesus promised his disciples that they would also receive power to do even greater deeds than he had done, and so they did.[3]

The advocates of "power evangelism" have again emphasized this point. They insist that there must be "supernatural" healings and exorcisms more powerful than the demonic powers that oppose the gospel to certify the gospel message. Certainly this insistence on a demonstration of God's power in Christ is correct. Especially in cultures that emphasize the supernatural and magical, it seems appropriate to demonstrate the power available through Christ in a mode which is familiar and recognized. The Christian message is not that we should replace "supernatural" means with "secular" remedies. By the same token, we need not insist on "supernatural" wonders to certify the gospel message in more scientifically oriented contexts.[4]

However, and this is our point, supernatural "wonders" outside the context of a "supernaturally" formed community of agape are quite ambiguous. The power of the Spirit is the power of love and life-affirming community. Within such a community of the Spirit, wonders of healing and reconciliation surely take place. Fear and shame are replaced by hope and respect. Manipulation, deceit, and depression, along with their physical symptoms, are healed. These are the hallmarks of the gospel.

The verbal announcement which accompanies the demonstrations of the power of agape takes the form of an explanation and invitation. We might paraphrase Jesus' words to the seventy as follows. "Exhibit the reality of the kingdom through action before you talk about it." Just as example should precede advice, so questions aroused by observation should precede the evangelistic answer.

Jesus' own example is illustrative. He awakened the question of his messianic identity by his extraordinary ministry long before he tried to explain to his disciples who he was. Similarly, Peter's sermon at Pentecost was a response to the questions of the crowd aroused by what was happening.

Again we are not urging thoroughly literal following of biblical examples. However, the relationship of act and explanation in evangelism is essential. The role of a witness is not argumentation and debate. Witnesses must depend on more than their good logic or rhetoric. The final appeal cannot be to some authority which will certify what is being said. Neither is the compulsion of mass suggestion acceptable. Only the authenticity and winsomeness of example, and the actuality of the healing, reconciling presence of the Spirit, can validate the witness.

Finally, the proclamation always implies an invitation. The gospel is like the announcement that dinner is ready. That means come and eat! Like the invitational announcements of graduations, weddings, or the opening of a new business, the gospel always includes an implicit RSVP. The gospel extends a call to leave the old and join the new community of the Spirit. And the form of the invitation is "Come and see." Such an invitation gives authenticity and credibility to the message.

The Community of Witness

The continuing witness of Jesus, the Christ, exists in the world as the messianic community. In Scripture the community is referred to as the "body of Christ," which is enlivened by his Spirit. This body is in the world as he was in the world.

In popular language, the messianic community has been called the "Jesus community," "Jesus people or family." While these designations often mean less than is intended by "messianic community," this language is helpful if we keep clearly in mind that Jesus came as the Messiah. Calling the community of witness the "Jesus community" gives it a concrete historical reference by relating it to Jesus' authenticating character and example. As Jesus himself bore witness to the kingdom of God, so the community continues to bear its witness.

Several important implications follow from this New Testament concept. First, the messianic community is the community under the Messiah's (Christ's) commission. The church is the servant of Jesus Christ for the world. The community of the Spirit is the community of Christ's Spirit. The Spirit is, as one theologian put it, Christ's "alter ego." Or as Luther said it, the Spirit is Christ's "vicar"—his authoritative representative—guiding and empowering the church for witness.

The community has been formed and deputized, as it were, to carry on the messianic mission. That is why it exists. Its mission gives it its form. A number of Christian communities have caught this vision of the centrality of mission in the life of the church. They have attempted to give it expression in the organization and life of the congregation.

Perhaps no community has worked at the messianic mission more deliberately over time than the Church of the Savior in Washington, D.C. In her book, *The New Community*, Elizabeth O'Connor, a member of the Church of the Savior, says community cannot truly participate in Christ unless it acts as an open, servant community identifying with the most needy of the world.

Taking this seriously, the original congregation of the Church of the Savior reconstituted itself into several sister communities, each organized around a specific mission. Individual spiritual discipline and group worship are fully integrated with Christlike service to the needy. In this way, the congregations work at holistic witness as a messianic community.

The "missionary mandate" is not a religious project of the church, to be assigned to a department or board of evangelism and fulfilled by individuals who go as "missionaries." Neither is it an altruistic gesture in which the community shares some of the blessings Christ has bestowed on it. The mission is not the fruit of benevolence or the largess of the church.

The mandate of Christ forms the community and gives it coherence. The community's purpose and methods, choice of priorities, style—all are determined by the messianic mandate. Its unity, or "catholicity," is found in the service of Christ. Only as the church loses itself in the quest for the "kingdom of God and his righteousness" will it gain authentic life.

Second, the community continues the basic stance of Christ's ministry and mission. Its fundamental character and purpose are not different from the ministry of Jesus.

What Jesus did as initiator of the new movement could only have been done by him. He did it "once for all." The mission of the messianic community is possible only because of what he did as "pioneer and perfecter of the faith." The messianic mission grows out of Jesus' ministry and follows it in time. It does not supersede his or substitute for Jesus' ministry. In this sense the community's ministry is not the repetition of Christ's ministry. It remains dependent on him as its authenticating witness.

But to the extent Jesus came to bear witness to and inaugurate a new era in the kingdom of God, the messianic community is the continuation of his ministry. He did not bring the rule of God to completion in his lifetime, not even in his resurrection. The kingdom of God is yet in an early stage, and the Messiah promised to return and complete what he began.

In the meantime, Christ has left a community of anticipation and witness to continue his introductory ministry. Thus the witnessing church continues to "share his sufferings, becoming like him in his death" (Phil. 3:10). It still prays, "Thy kingdom come, thy will be done on earth as it is in heaven."

The kingdom of God is the reality of which the church is a sign. To speak of the church as a sign is to describe it as a kind of evidence (witness). The church is an indicator having an intrinsic relation with that to which it points. The church is that community which already recognizes the rule of God through the lordship of Christ. Only as an authentic sign can it be a credible witness.

Thus the church continues its witness as an anticipatory sign of the coming salvation and rule of God. It exists in the world, although not of the world, as a community of God's peace. Under God's rule it is concerned for *all* life—spiritual, social, physical—and it defines evangelism as holistic witness, not simply verbal proclamation.

The Voice of Calvary ministries in Mendenhall and Jackson, Mississippi, are an example of holistic mission. John Perkins, its founder, soon discovered that in the African-American community evangelistic preaching alone was inadequate to communicate the gospel. He had to flesh it out in ministries of social and political activity. Poverty, injustice, and exploitation had to be dealt with in the name of the gospel.

Such ministries involved Perkins and his congregation with both church and nonchurch members alike. The witness was corporate and identifiable as the church making disciples, but its activities and its strategy thrust it into the world without sharply defined "churchly" and "parachurchly" organizations and functions. Its evangelistic witness called individuals to faith and discipleship, and simultaneously challenged the demonic structures of racism which controlled both secular and religious Mississippi institutions.

Witness as Dialogue

David Lochhead has argued persuasively that "dialogical relationship" is the only proper stance for agape witness. He points out that dialogue should not be defined in such a way that it rules out "proclamation" in the New Testament meaning of that word. The dialogical relationship is "marked by openness, honesty, and search for understanding" (1988:85). One does not have to step outside such a relationship to witness.

Lochhead contrasts "dialogue" with "monologue," and argues that the Christian witness is not monological. "The commandment to love one's neighbor as Christ has loved us translates for the Christian into the dialogical imperative, the imperative to seek dialogue and to be open to dialogue whenever and from whomever it is offered" (1988:81).

The idea of interreligious dialogue as a form of witness has been suspect in the evangelical community. This is partly because dialogue as defined by some of its more liberal advocates rules out the Christian's presupposition that Jesus Christ is the ultimate truth and Savior of the world. According to this definition, one must enter dialogue in a mutual search for truth. Thus to make dialogue a means to convert the partner subverts the process. Nevertheless, as Harold Netland points out in his latest book, *Dissonant Voices*, there are a number of areas where dialogue with other ideologies and religious groups can be helpful (1991:283-301).

Evangelicalism's suspicion of dialogue has also been due in part to its understanding of evangelism as a monological announcement. Orthodoxy, both Roman Catholic and Protestant, has consistently viewed its mission in terms of a "crusade." It has gone forth with the assumption that it is fighting an "evil empire"— "Turks," "Papacy," "Jews," "Communists." Other cultures are heathen and demonic; other religions are false; other objects of worship (gods) are idols and enemies of true faith. In such a frame of mind, any attempt at genuine dialogue seems a compromise. For example, some early Baptist missionaries to India refused to study Hindu culture with the retort, "We did not come to study the work of the devil but to destroy it!"

We can appreciate the passionate loyalty of such missionaries to Jesus Christ as Lord, but the hostility to other religious cultures smacks of unbecoming arrogance and imperialism.[5] As Lochhead observes,

> There is here [in the dialogical imperative] an important issue for evangelical Christianity, and one that ought not to be minimized. The question, put abstractly, is how the self-giving of Christ is made known to people of other religious traditions and how their response is invited" (1991:80).

The incarnation clearly implies a dialogical relationship between God and the world of humanity. Jesus came as servant (Mark 10:45), and washed his disciples' feet (John 13:1-17). The true "Word became flesh and lived among us." The incarnation implies that God respects and makes himself vulnerable to the human race. He opened himself to learn what it meant to be a human in first-century Jewish culture. That is the stance of dialogue.

Paul voices the principle of dialogical relationship when he says, "I am a debtor both to Greeks and to barbarians, both to the wise and to the foolish" (Rom. 1:14). And when he says, "I have become all things to all people, that I might by all means save some" (1 Cor. 9:22). Paul's attitude and approach toward those of other religious communities is more clearly implied in Romans 2, where he says God shows no partiality, and everyone's standing before God is a matter of grace, not affiliation with the right religion (vv. 12-16, 28-29).

It is true that Paul is pessimistic in his estimate of human ability to achieve salvation apart from the grace of God revealed in Christ. We should not, however, confuse this with a comparative evaluation of various religions. It is a mistake to interpret Romans 1:18-32 as a broadside against all nonbiblical religions.

Paul is precise in stating what and whom he is criticizing, namely, all "those who by their [ungodliness and] wickedness suppress the truth" (v.18). From what follows it is clear that this category can also include such people in the tradition of biblical religion as well as others. When Paul speaks about Christian warfare, he says we fight spiritual powers, not other religions and cultures. He did not wage a crusade against heathen cultures.

Paul's dialogical style shines through in Luke's account of his missionary approach. Paul approached the Jewish community with great respect, addressing them as "my brothers" (Acts 13:26). He addressed the Greeks who showed interest in Judaism as those "who fear God." In the Christian community itself, he argued against a culturally superior attitude implied in the Judaizers' refusal to eat with Gentiles.

Perhaps the clearest example of Paul's dialogical approach is found in his address on Mars Hill (Acts 17). Here, in a bid for dialogue, Paul complimented them on their religious concern, appealed to a local legend about salvation from a plague to introduce his own kerygmatic announcement, and quoted from their Greek poets with approval to underscore his point.[6]

In this day of competing religious and secular ideologies—such as capitalism versus socialism, liberalism versus fundamentalism, Islam versus Judaism, Protestantism versus Catholicism—we must remind ourselves that the gospel is not an ideology. It is the story of what has happened both in past history and in our own lives. The New Testament word translated "preach" or "proclaim" (words that may suggest monologue) is *kerygma*. The kerygma is the telling of a story, and, as Lochhead reminds us, a story is dialogical in form. It does not argue; it simply informs and invites the partner to "participate actively. Story both engages the imagination of the listener and leaves the listener free" (1991:86).

Dialogue does not rule out conviction, explanation, or even persuasion. To be taken seriously in a dialogue one must have a clear self-identity and intelligent convictions. Mutual explanation and questioning is the essential form of dialogue. And when one is convinced of the truth of one's position, sharing that position implies desire to persuade. However, the temptation is to use pressure and even to manipulate to persuade. It is at this point that dialogue turns into monologue. And here the witness to grace must take the Holy Spirit's role in dialogue seriously. Jesus said that it is the Spirit's task to convict (John 15:26-27; 16:8-11).

In contrast to monologue, where one person speaks and the other person listens, a dialogue takes place where people listen and speak to each other. Listening is a primary and indispensable part of dialogue. In the monological stance, the "superior" one knows and speaks, the "inferior" one is ignorant and listens.

Proper humility and respect for the partner in conversation is imperative in dialogue. The monological stance is argumentative. The debater aims to prove a point and "win" the debate. The dialogical stance is informative and confessional. The witness aims to win the confidence of the partner through a sincere, honest relationship.[7]

In a period of history when religious fundamentalisms—Hindu, Islamic, Christian, Shinto—have again become major rivals on the international scene, it is important to underscore this dialogical character of the witness to grace. The gospel, as Paul says, is the power of God to reconcile alienated factions and free us all from self-serving behavior. Grace enables and invites. It never coerces or manipulates. The church, as the community of the Holy Spirit and the sign of the gracious rule of God, is constantly challenged to give an authentic witness to this grace.

Notes

Chapter 1: Pentecost and the Gospel

1. See J. W. Bowman, "The Term 'Gospel' and Its Cognates in the Palestinian Syriac" (Higgins, 1959:54-67). He argues that it has both a religious and secular usage.

2. Friedrich has an excellent statement of this dimension of *gospel* in his TDNT article on *euangelion*: "The Gospel does not merely bear witness to a historical event, for what it recounts, namely, resurrection and exaltation, is beyond the scope of historical judgment and transcends history. Nor does it consist only of narratives and sayings concerning Jesus which every Christian must know, and it certainly does not consist in a dogmatic formula alien to the world. On the contrary, it is related to human reality and proves itself to be living power. . . . The Gospel does not merely bear witness to salvation history; it is itself salvation history. It breaks into the life of man, refashions it and creates communities" (Kittel, 1964:731).

3. Donald Baillie has developed this point in a most insightful way in his *God Was in Christ*, Scribners, 1948, pp. 153-54.

4. F. D. Bruner has a splendid discussion of this passage, but as usual he is aiming pietistic guns at pentecostal positions and fails to consider that more than personal enduement is at stake (1970:155ff.).

5. G. W. H. Lampe speaks of Pentecost as "the great turning point in history" (p. 192). See his "The Holy Spirit in the Writings of St. Luke" (Nineham, 1955:159-200).

6. See Maurice Barnett, *The Living Flame*, 1953; Otto Piper, "Exodus in the New Testament," *Interpretation* (January 1957), pp. 3-22; and Harold Sahlin, "The New Exodus of Salvation According to St. Paul" (Fridrichsen, ed., 1953:81ff.). Flew writes, "To the question: 'What happened at Pentecost?' we may answer, a fresh revelation of God's activity in the present, which resulted not only in a new experience of God through Christ in the lives of all believers, but a new quality of fellowship" (1943:109).

7. Although the written rabbinic source of this tradition is later than the *Acts* account, it may well have been oral tradition prior to that. At any rate, it gives an authentic clue to the symbolism. See Kee, Young, and Froelich, 1965:306.

8. Ernest Stoeffler says that they were attempting to "capture the meaning of the early Koinonia" (1965:160).

9. Lycurgus Starkey gives a fine exposition of this theology and experience *The Work of the Holy Spirit* (Abingdon, 1962).

10. See B. B. Warfield, "The Cessation of the Charismata," (1953:1-32).

11. Vinson Synan has made this distinction very clear in his *The Holiness Pentecostal Movement* (1971).

12. See the next chapter for an expansion of the biblical data on the relation of the individual to the community. Clearly the indivdual finds his or her self-identity in community.

13. The theologians of the Reformation worked with the opposing categories of *Bible* and *Spirit*, *law* and *grace*. Even the Anabaptist leaders by and large accepted these categories of Luther. Consequently in their emphasis upon conversion and new life, they tended toward biblical literalism and the interpretation of the New Testament as a new law which by the grace of God can and should be obeyed. Calvin's biblicism and reinforcement of the Spirit's motivation with institutional sanctions is well attested.

14. The term "social contract" actually comes from Rousseau.

15. Sidney Mead has given an insightful analysis of the character of American denominationalism in his book *The Lively Experiment* (1963). See especially chapter VII. Claude Welch refers to the Protestant notion of the church as a "voluntaristic association" and points out that it was characteristic of conservatives and liberals alike (1958:31ff.). In their sociological analysis, *Habits of the Heart*, Robert Bellah and his associates write of the relation of the individual to the church and note the difficulty modern Americans have in recognizing the organic priority and authority of the church as community (chap. 9, especially pp. 235ff.).

16. H. W. Robinson says, "If we ask what is the most characteristic and comprehensive work of the Holy Spirit, according to the New Testament, there can be little doubt that we should answer in the one word, 'fellowship' [*koinonia*]" (1928/58:141). Again, he says, "Where there is no fellowship with all its brotherly activities, he [the outsider] sees no true church" (p. 146).

Chapter 2: Biblical Perspectives on the Individual-in-Community

1. This individualistic stance is vividly portrayed in the idealized body language of Protestant worship. Individual worshipers sit in long rows with heads bowed, eyes closed, and hands clasped in silent reverence before God in the church of their choice.

2. For a number of reasons, most of which grow out of historical circumstances in the last century, this issue of the individual in community has become a highly sensitive one for conservative American Protestants. Terms like social gospel, socialism, communalism, and especially communism immediately raise red flags. For this reason it is advisable for me to explicitly point out that I have no design in this chapter to defend any political system by the Bible. In any case, communism as it has been developed in Russia, Eastern Europe, and China represents a *collectivization*, not an organic community. Neither do I espouse the liberal Social Gospel of the early twentieth century. However, I do believe that there are social dimen-

sions to the gospel that have been overlooked and neglected in conservative Protestantism.

3. For extended studies of the biblical doctrine of humanity see Stuart Barton Babbage, *Man in Nature and in Grace*, Eerdmans, 1957; Walther Eichrodt, *Man in the Old Testament*, Alec R. Allenson, 1951; Russell Shedd, *Man in Community*, Eerdmans, 1964; G. Ernest Wright, *The Biblical Doctrine of Man in Society*, SCM, 1954.

4. The concept of "corporate personality" was introduced into Old Testament studies by the famous Baptist scholar, H. Wheeler Robinson, in the early part of this century. See his *Christian Doctrine of Man*, and articles like "Corporate Personality in Ancient Israel" (1935, reissued as a Facet Book, 1964), and "The Group and the Individual in Ancient Israel" (1937). More recently this idea has been sharply challenged by some biblical scholars. See, for example, G. E. Mendenhall, "The Relation of the Individual to Political Society in Ancient Israel," *Biblical Studies in Memory of H. C. Alleman*, ed. by J. M. Myers, J. J. Augustin Publishers, 1960; J. R. Porter, "The Legal Aspects of the Concept of 'Corporate Personality' in the Old Testament," *Vetus Testamentum*, XI (July 1965), 361-380; and J. W. Rogerson, "The Hebrew Conception of Corporate Personality: A Re-examination," *Journal of Theological Studies*, XXI (April 1970), 1-16.

5. In a similar fashion, the Japanese phrases *jibun no aru* and *jibun no nai* (literally to have or not have a self) speak of a relation to the family or clan unit. One who has been ostracized has lost selfhood. See Takeo Doi, *The Anatomy of Dependence*, Harper & Row, 1973, 132ff.

6. Aristotle held that the highest specimen of humanity is the self-sufficient, male philosopher.

7. See Walther Eichrodt, *Man in the Old Testament*, (1951), pp. 13ff., for an extended discussion of this material.

8. E. F. Scott, in *Man and Society in the New Testament* (Scribners, 1947), held that "it was Jesus who first discovered that every man is a person with value and destiny of his own" (83). This seems to be too strong a statement of the point in light of our review of the Old Testament materials. Jesus stands in continuity with the prophets in this respect. Scott's liberal individualistic bias seems to have influenced his interpretation of Jesus and hence the contrast to the Old Testament.

9. It is inconceivable that Jesus could have come to self-consciousness as the Messiah outside the Jewish community. His cultural context made his identity crisis and its resolution distinct from the enlightenment of the Buddha, for example.

10. I do not intend here negative assessment of Jesus' status as Son of God. That is a theological issue and at the moment I am attempting to make a psychological point about the man, Jesus.

11. In this passage Paul actually uses the word "sonship," but this is not sexist favoritism. He applies the metaphor of sonship to all believers, male and female. In the first-century culture it was the sons who had legal family status—freedom and inheritance—and it is this "sonship" status which now

belongs to all in God's family.

12. The unavoidable implication of Dispensationalist theology, which makes a Jewish, Palestinian kingdom the final historical goal of the Messiah and the fulfillment of the Abrahamic covenant, is that *law* and *nationalism* are God's final words in history! The kingdom of God on earth becomes a universal messianic political system administered under a "rule of law."

13. While this relation to the community is not formally different from the Jews' relation through identification as a child of the Law, the radical difference is that law cannot transcend community as a living person does. The prophetic experience is the precursor of the new relationship. In the name of Yahweh the prophets challenged the community's understanding and use of the Law.

14. These quotations are taken from Fritjof Capra's explanation of Ken Wilber's "spectrum psychology." (*The Turning Point*, Toronto/ New York: Bantam Books, 1983, 371.) Douglas R. Groothuis, *Unmasking the New Age* (InterVarsity, 1986), and Russell Chandler, *Understanding the New Age* (Word, 1988) both provide a good introduction to New Age thought.

Chapter 3: Jesus and the Community

1. Flew, Jesus and His Church (revised edition, 1943) went through many printings, and remains a fruitful study. Flew believes we can know something of Jesus' thought about the church. He argues that the *ekklēsia* is the necessary correlative to the *basileia*, or kingly rule of God which Jesus preached. Gerhard Lohfink, *Jesus and Community* (1984) argues that Jesus' main concern was not with the individual and private salvation, but with the restoration of Israel as the eschatological people of God. Raymond Brown's Sprunt Lectures (1980) were published by the Paulist Press in 1984 under the title *The Churches the Apostles Left Behind*. He compares and contrasts the different church traditions of the late first century as they are reflected in the epistles and gospels of the New Testament.

2. Martin Hengel, *Studies in the Gospel of Mark* (1985:53). Compare C. F. D. Moule, *The Gospel According to Mark* (1965:8).

3. In his article, "The Church in Matthew," James Martin agrees. "For Matthew, the life of the church is above all else discipleship. . . . The crucial matter for the church of Matthew is not whether or not there should be a charismatic ministry but whether or not there shall be a complete and perfect discipleship which combines charismatic activities and ethical obedience to Jesus' interpretation of the Law in his word and deed. . . . The church lives by the Sermon on the Mount, not in the abstract or in a legalistic way, but as the community which knows its origins in the promise of Jesus formulated as the Beatitudes, and which understands the Law as a living tradition concerning God's will interpreted by Jesus" (Mays, 1987:105, 106, 107).

4. Oscar Cullmann gives a good summary of the long and tortuous debate about the meaning of this passage. See *Peter* (1962:165-176). He follows with his own interpretation of the passage.

5. Flew has an excellent commentary on the meaning of the keys. "The

key of the kingdom is here the 'knowledge' which makes entrance to the kingdom possible. . . . It is insight into the meaning of the final Messianic salvation, and is linked with the idea of forgiveness of sins. This 'key' therefore is far more than intellectual knowledge. . . . The key is the spiritual insight which will enable Peter to lead others in through the door of revelation through which he has passed himself" (1943:95).

6. This same conviction is expressed in Ephesians 3:10, where it is said that God wants to make his plan known to the rulers of the world through the church.

7. James Martin has written, "For both evangelists (Matthew and Luke) . . . the time of Jesus and the time of the church belong together eschatologically, because both Gospels are witness to the resurrection of Jesus; and it is the reality of the living Lord of the church which enables them to write the kind of history they present in the Gospels" (Mays, 1987:98).

8. Some ancient manuscripts say *seventy* and some *seventy-two*. E. J. Tinsley explains. "Seventy, in the number symbolism of Judaism, was a conventional figure for all the nations of the world. . . . *Seventy-two* is the number given in the Greek translation of the Hebrew Old Testament . . . for the nations of the world in Gen. 10. . . . Most probably this [seventy-two] is the original reading, and 'seventy' crept in later because of its more common use as a symbol for something universal." *The Gospel According to Luke* (1965:113).

9. Raymond E. Brown, *The Community of the Beloved Disciple* (1979, 13).

10. See his "Excursus 17: 'The Disciples, the Community and the Church in the Gospel of John,' " (1990:203-217).

11. T. W. Manson equates the "remnant" in Isaiah with the "suffering servant." "For him the whole community which has survived the Exile is to be the Servant of Jehovah, and to realize in itself the ideal represented in the Songs." He points out that those who recognized Jesus as the Messiah were the continuation of this remnant, this servant community—the true Israel. *The Teachings of Jesus* (1963: 176-181, 189-190).

12. Schnackenburg agrees. "Jesus' death and the Christian proclamation of that death lead directly to the formation of the community of salvation. Anyone who wishes to belong to that community has to make a decision of faith" (1990:215). There is also an allusion to this relation of Jesus' death and the spread of his mission in the question of Jesus' opponents in 7:35-36. When Jesus speaks of his coming death as a "going away" where they cannot find him, they wonder whether he would go to the Jews in the Hellenistic dispersion.

13. A. M. Hunter's *The Message of the New Testament* includes an excellent chapter entitled "Jesus and the Church" (pp. 52-66), which argues that the church is implicit not only in Jesus' teaching but in his action.

14. In his article on *ekklēsia* K. L. Schmidt quotes Linton approving. "The Messiah is not a private person. A community belongs to Him. The flock belongs to the Shepherd" (TDNT, III, 521 n.).

Chapter 4: The Apostolic Community

1. Hengel states, "The earliest [church] community in Palestine was also a missionary community from the beginning: the foundation for this lies in the sending by the Risen Christ." And he adds that the "real starting point of the primitive Christian mission . . . lies in the conduct of Jesus himself. If anyone is to be called 'the primal missionary,' he must be" (1983:62-63).

2. Inasmuch as we will be using terms like movement, society, and sect frequently, it may be best to offer some definitions. A *society* is an *organizationally* defined association which forms on the basis of compatibility or agreed-upon regulations and goals. It is constituted by its organizational structure. While a society may be activity- or project-oriented and altruistic in its purposes, it exists for the members, i.e., for accomplishing their purposes and for whatever other advantages may come with membership.

A *club* has essentially the same character except that it generally is more oriented toward the self-fulfillment of the group.

A *sect* or *denomination* is a religious society in the above sense. The standards for membership are adherence to an agreed-upon religious faith and practice, compatibility with and willingness to support the purposes of the organization. It seeks to perpetuate itself as an organized community through acquiring new members and thus to carry on its altruistic purposes.

A *movement* is less structured, more heterogeneous and flexible than a society. It is not organizationally defined. Rather, it gains its character and structure from the purpose for which it exists, i.e., its mission. But what is probably more significant is its relation to the whole (larger) group within which it operates. A movement aims to effect changes in the larger social order. It does not exist to perpetuate itself as a movement, but to bring its purposes to realization within the whole social order of which it is a part.

3. John Howard Yoder writes, "This new Christian community in which the walls are broken down not by human idealism or democratic legalism but by the work of Christ is not only a vehicle of the gospel or fruit of the gospel; it is the good news. It is not merely the agent of mission or the constituency of a mission agency. This is the mission." ("A People in the World: Theological Interpretation," in Garrett, 1969:274.) Howard Snyder, who refers to Yoder's article, writes, "If Jesus Christ actually gave more time to preparing a community of disciples than to proclaiming the good news (which he did), then the contemporary Church must also recognize the importance of community for proclamation" (1977:74).

4. See Kraus, *Dispensationalism in America: Its Rise and Development*, John Knox, 1958; Rowden, *The Origins of the Brethren 1825-1850*, Pickering and Inglis Ltd., 1967; and Ernest R. Sandeen, *The Roots of Fundamentalism, British and American Millenarianism 1800-1930*, University of Chicago, 1970.

5. It was a happy omen when the late F. F. Bruce, who was of Plymouth Brethren background, wrote in his commentary that he could adopt the words of C. H. Dodd with only "one qualification." (Dodd taught that the

kingdom was "realized" in the coming of the Spirit at Pentecost.) Bruce wrote, "Biblical eschatology is largely, but not completely, 'realized': there still remains a future element, to become actual at the Second Advent, the *parousia*. A balanced account of the NT presentation of the kingdom of God requires that due regard be paid to both of these aspects" (1954:35-36).

Oscar Cullmann introduced the language of "already and not yet." He wrote, "The *new element in the New Testament is not eschatology, but what I call the tension* between the decisive 'already fulfilled' and the 'not yet completed,' between present and future. The whole theology of the New Testament, including Jesus' preaching, is qualified by this tension." *Salvation in History*, 1967:172.

6. Two excellent studies of the social implications of Jesus' kingdom teachings: John H. Yoder's *The Politics of Jesus* (Eerdmans, 1972), and Donald Kraybill's *The Upside-Down Kingdom* (Herald Press, 1990 revised edition). Howard Snyder in *The Community of the King* (1977) wrestles with the relation of church and kingdom, and how the growth of the one can affect the other. (See especially chapter 7, "Church Growth and Kingdom Growth.")

7. T. W. Manson, *The Teaching of Jesus* (1963:190).

8. Beginning with the publication of George E. Ladd's *Crucial Questions About the Kingdom of God* (1952), there has been a gradual shift away from the dispensationalist position in evangelical circles. See Peter Kuzmic, "The Church and the Kingdom of God" (Nicholls, 1968:49-81), and Everett F. Harrison, *The Apostolic Church* (Eerdmans, 1985).

9. See Jordan's *The Cotton Patch Version of Matthew and John* (Association Press, 1970). Koinonia Farm was an attempt to translate the kingdom values into personal and social reality. It was a Christian community where consumerism, capitalistic competition, racial discrimination were submitted to kingdom values. Out of it has come the well-known project of Habitat for Humanity which attempts to make affordable housing available to the poor.

10. This concept of God Movement may be compared to the idea of *missio Dei* which has come into use since the late 1950s in the world missionary discussions. See J. Verkuyl, *Contemporary Missiology : An Introduction*, 1978:3 for an introduction to the term.

11. Since I first wrote these words in the early 1970s, much has been written on the church's position in the world. Charles Scriven's *The Transformation of Culture* (Herald, 1988) is of particular interest. He argues that H. Richard Niebuhr's position of "Christ transforming culture" (*Christ and Culture*, 1951) is correct, but the Anabaptist strategy for the church in the world is the New Testament way. The nonviolent community faithful to the vision of Jesus for a transformed world must function as "alternative society" and "transformative example" (pp. 181ff.). Note also Adeyemo Tokunboh, "The Church and Its Mandate for Social Change" (Nicholls, 1968:163:180).

The actual way in which a movement operates in its environing social order is historically conditioned. Sometimes it must exist underground as in the early church. Sometimes it may function openly as part of a democratic process as in Western culture today. The important thing is that it should not misunderstand its mission.

12. I have elaborated this point in reference to health care in *The Healing Christ* (Herald Press, 1972).

13. Secular, as I have indicated, means first of all temporal or historical. My point here is made if we contrast religious or sacred to secular. The church must see itself as a part of the "everyday," "this-worldly" life of humanity. This was the main thrust of Colin Williams' two essays, *Where in the World?* and *What in the World?* (National Council of Churches, 1963, 1964).

14. Menno Simons has written, "For true evangelical faith is of such a nature that it cannot lie dormant, but manifests itself in all righteousness and works of love. . . . It clothes the naked; it feeds the hungry; it comforts the sorrowful; it shelters the destitute; it aids and consoles the sad; it returns good for evil; it serves those that harm it; it prays for those that persecute it; teaches, admonishes, and reproves with the Word of the Lord. . ." ("Why I Do Not Cease Teaching and Writing," Wenger, 1956:307.)

15. In *The Racial Problem in Christian Perspective* (1959), Kyle Haselden points out that the signs "White" and "Colored" were posted in the churches before they were posted in public facilities. In the beginning of the Pentecostal movement in the United States, the gospel overcame segregation, but in the period 1914-1925 the churches capitulated to the segregation laws that forbad Christians to worship together.

16. "Human Values: The Crisis in the Congregation," *International Review of Missions* (January 1971, pp. 70-80). I have slightly reworded for my purposes.

17. The Anabaptists, who reintroduced the believers church in the Reformation, were ardent evangelists calling people into the true church. They were conscious, however, that the activity of God is not limited to the church and that his rule extends over all humans whether they recognize Christ or not. Therefore, while not confusing the role of church and government, they confronted magistrates with the biblical requirements for their office. Menno Simons is a good example of this. For an example see "Foundation of Christian Doctrine" (*Complete Works*, pp. 204-205).

18. See Langdon Gilkey, *How the Church Can Minister to the World Without Losing Itself* (1964), especially chapter 3, for an excellent discussion. He writes, "Some form of the social gospel is a requirement for a holy church in the world, lest it capitulate entirely to the world and lose its own being" (p. 71). See also Tullio Vinay's article, " 'Servizio Cristiano' in Riesi, Sicily," *International Review of Missions*, January 1973, p. 66. Vinay is a Waldensian Christian who established a community among the poor of Sicily.

Chapter 5: The Saved and Saving Community

1. See L. S. Chafer, *Systematic Theology*, Vol. VII, Dallas Seminary (1948) for an example of this kind of definition.

I have moved rather quickly from the Reformers themselves to positions that developed in the following centuries. Calvin himself gives relatively more significance to membership in the visible church. He discusses the church under the heading of "External Means of Grace." The visible church is for the "motherly care" and "nourishment" of those who by a "secret election and inner call" belong to the true, invisible church. "But because a small and contemptible number are hidden in a huge multitude and a few grains of wheat are covered by a pile of chaff, we must leave to God alone the knowledge of his church, whose foundation is his secret election" (*Institutes of the Christian Religion*, IV, 1, 2. Vol. 2, p. 1013).

2. Menno wrote: "For if we had the spirit, faith, and power of Zacchaeus, which we verily should have . . . there would soon be a different and better situation because, it cannot fail, *the righteous must live his faith*" (Wenger, 1956:369). See also his discussion of justification in "Distressed Christians" on pages 503-508.

3. Franklin Littell develops this in his *A Tribute to Menno*, (1961:23-36).

4. George Barna, *What Americans Believe* (Regal, 1991). Barna's findings are substantiated by the polls of Andrew M. Greeley, George Gallup, Jr., and others. *Newsweek* (December 17, 1990) reported on the return of the "Baby Boomers" to the churches, but it noted the changed character in the churches. "This is the 1990s, an age of mix 'em, match 'em salad-bar spirituality—Quakerpalians, charismatic Catholics, New Age Jews—where brand loyalty is a doctrine of the past and the customer is king" (p. 50). In its January 6, 1992, issue *Newsweek* featured a report of research on attitudes and practice of prayer in America. It reports that 91% of women and 85% of men pray, and 78% of all Americans pray at least once a week (pp. 39ff.).

5. Matthew presents the Sermon on the Mount in a more formal way as the new covenant law. Luke gives it as an essential characterization of the new community of forgiveness. In both accounts the sermon is integral to forming of the new disciple community.

6. The "kingdom of God" is synonymous with the Old Testament "salvation of Yahweh." It designates the end of alienation and hostility against God's rule. From Matthew's use of the phrase in 19:16-30, it is synonymous with being saved and inheriting eternal life. Note how this language is used interchangeably.

7. *Beyond Freedom and Dignity* (Knopf, 1971). See especially chapters 2 and 4.

8. In *On Earth As in Heaven* (Herald Press, 1991), Arthur Paul Boers maintains that the contemplative life is the ground and nurturing source for active service, not an alternative to it.

9. We owe this insight on the post-Pentecost community network to André Trocmé, *Jesus and the Nonviolent Revolution* (1974).

10. Flew argues that "the word *koinonia* seems to be never used as equivalent to a community, or *societas*. The dominant sense of the word is the inner relationship which constitutes fellowship" (1943:109-10). Certainly Flew is correct in suggesting that the word does not indicate a particular so-

ciological form, but rather the inner dynamic. However, the word *community* carries that double meaning, and to speak of the community as a *koinonia* points to the mutual relationship rather than the form.

11. I first heard this kind of language among the blacks in the civil rights movement in the 1960s. As they gained a new sense of self-worth, they reminded each other "You is somebody!"

12. For a fuller discussion see Heinrich Bornkamm, *Luther's World of Thought* (1965:134 ff.).

Chapter 6: The Gospel of Peace

1. See Ray Abrams, *Preachers Present Arms* (Herald Press, 1969). It is interesting to note how evangelical scholars of the 1970s and 80s made the case for violence in virtually the same terms as Reinhold Niebuhr, who argued the case for using violence in the public order based on a liberal hermeneutic.

2. See for example the works of Jim Wallis and the Sojourner Community; Ronald Sider's, *Christ and Violence* (Herald Press, 1979), and Walter Wink, *Naming the Powers* and *Unmasking the Powers* (Fortress Press), and *Violence and Nonviolence in South Africa: Jesus' Third Way* (New Society Publishers, 1987).

3. See Kraus, *Jesus Christ Our Lord* (1990:154-156).

4. In his article, "The Apostle Paul and the Introspective Conscience of the West" (*Harvard Theological Review*, 1963:202f.), Krister Stendahl noted that Luther was nearer to Augustine than to Paul. "Apparently Paul did not have the type of introspective conscience which such a formula [*simul justus et peccator*] seems to presuppose." He notes that Augustine was one of the first to express such a conscience and says further, "In these matters Luther was a truly Augustinian monk."

5. Eric Wahlstrom, a Lutheran scholar, has challenged the application of categories such as "Christ mysticism" to Paul. He makes a solid case for the moral character of the "in Christ" idiom (*The New Life in Christ*, 1950).

6. The term "social contract" is usually associated with Rousseau, who was dependent upon the English philosopher John Locke for much of his political thought. Locke proposed it as the only way to regulate the selfish interests of human beings. In place of authority which is based upon despotic power, he advocated enlightened self-interest. According to Locke, government exists to protect private property.

7. The Puritans and other early settlers in America assumed they were God's chosen ones, and that this gave them the right to take the land from native Americans. This assumption also underlaid the justification for enslaving the blacks. It remains implicit in the arguments of the children of the Puritans to this day.

8. A. M. Hunter says we might paraphrase the fourth beatitude: "Blessed are those who ardently desire the vindication of the right, and triumph of the good cause." He suggests that "righteousness" in Matthew 6:33 has the same meaning (*A Pattern for Life*, 1953:34, 81).

9. Gandhi taught that noncooperation with systemic evil which dominates in human society is just as important as cooperation with the right.

10. This has been a constant implicit assumption in the history of American churches. In the last decades of the nineteenth century, for example, church leaders often identified the task of missions as "Christianization," in which they included democratization and free trade. At the end of World War II, Carl McIntire preached a crusade against communism in which he equated freedom in Christ with political freedom as it is known in America (*Author of Liberty*, Christian Beacon Press, 1946). This was an extreme but consistent example of this kind of thinking. And even today John Foster Dulles, who rallied the "free world" in a cold war to "contain communism," is still revered by many as the great *Christian* statesman of this century.

Chapter 7: The Spirit of Love

1. C. S. Lewis, *Four Loves* (1960), discusses *eros*.

2. William Phipps suggests that *agape* is the word used in the Septuagint (LXX) and this accounts for New Testament usage. He points out that the word covers a broad range of meanings in the New Testament. ("The Sensuousness of Agape," *Theology Today*, January 1973, 370-379.)

3. Benevolent Empire was the name given to the large network of charitable institutions and movements for the improvement of society which developed alongside of and as a result of the Second Great Awakening.

4. This is the meaning of Jesus' words, "Let them deny themselves and take up their cross" (Mark 8:34, NRSV). The word translated "deny" really means "lose sight of self," so the passage might be better translated, "Let them stop looking at things from a selfish perspective."

5. I have discussed the nature of *agape* in *Jesus Christ Our Lord* (1991) on pages 142 ff., and 164-166.

6. See Robert Handy, "The Christian Conquest of the World," in *A Christian America: Protestant Hopes and Historical Realities* (1971:117-154).

7. During America's war with Vietnam, the Area Secretary for Southeast Asia of the Christian and Missionary Alliance sent a release to all official workers in North America. The C M A had a vigorous network of churches in the country at the time and sympathized with America's military action. The secretary wrote: "May I encourage you to continue in prayer for the situation [Vietnam war]. The outcome of a communist takeover of South Vietnam would undoubtedly be that both Cambodia and Laos would quickly succumb to communist elements. Thailand would probably opt for either a pro-communist stance, or perhaps a neutralism similar to that found in Burma. In either event, it would likely signal the end of Christian missionary endeavor. *I cannot believe that it is in God's providence or purpose that an additional fifty-six million people be sealed off from free access to the message of the gospel. . . .*" [Italics mine]

Chapter 8: The Community's Witness to Grace

1. I have used the word community throughout the essay, but the word

city (*polis*) would be almost equally acceptable if we understood the connotation of that word in the ancient world. The city was the center of civilized
life. It was the symbol of political order, where life was humanized. It was
the center of commerce and therefore abundance. Behind its walls was security against invaders. Thus it early became a symbol of God's work in history as well as of human achievement in defiance of God. We are told that
in contrast to the wealthy cities of ancient Chaldea, Abraham looked for a
city built by God (Heb. 11:10; cf. 12:22). Revelation 18-21 describes the final destruction of the city of Babylon (the defiant human city) and the de-
scent of the heavenly city in glorious beauty. Within that city, whose twelve
foundations symbolize the twelve apostles, flows the river of life beside
which stands a tree of life on either side. The light of the city is Christ himself, and "by its light shall the nations walk." This is simply a highly symbolic description of the consummated community of salvation.

2. The charismatic movement, which began to be prominent in the
1960s, has again emphasized the relation of experience and power to witness. They accentuate the spiritual *power of the message itself*, which is not the
power of rhetoric or logic. For example, Rodman Williams says that Peter's
speech "immediately" after the outpouring of the Spirit "was not the same
as before Pentecost. It was now laden with power—spiritual power. It was
not great oratory or 'enticing words of man's wisdom,' but it was in 'tongues
of fire' lighted by the Holy Spirit" (1972:94). The stress of the charismatics
is an individual experience of the Spirit's power.

See also David Shibley, *A Force in the Earth, The Charismatic Renewal and
World Evangelism* (1989), and C. Peter Wagner, *Spiritual Power and Church
Growth* (1986). Wagner mentions that the Pentecostals of South America
tied their "power evangelism" into church nurture and membership.
Largely, however, the emphasis has been on the supernatural power to
heal and cast out demons. Compare the work of John Wimber in Vineyard
Ministries International who has brought the "power evangelism" into
prominence among non-Pentecostals.

3. John Calvin's explanation is that the signs of God's power are no
longer necessary since Christendom has been established. This looks like
an excuse, although he was undoubtedly sincere in his belief. Such emphasis on the power of the Word alone has been characteristic of modern evangelicalism until the breakthrough of Pentecostalism and the Charismatic
movement challenged the interpretation of miracles as a first-century-only
phenomenon.

4. The question is not whether a transcendent God is at work through
the gospel. Rather it is how God works in the variety of human contexts to
authenticate his presence and salvation. Physical wonders in themselves,
whether of science, magic, or supernatural power, cannot authenticate the
gospel of *shalom* and *agape*.

5. Lochhead describes four common ideologies that have defined the
relation of Christianity and other religious communities. (1) "Isolation,"
which does not take other religions seriously, and devalues their genuine-

ness. (2) "Hostility," which views them as threatening and sees the mission in terms of attack. (3) "Competition," which considers that they and the Christian religion are "in the same business," but assumes the superiority and final conquest of Christianity over them. (4) "Partnership," which assumes that all religions have a common referent, and are in a common search for reality. The last is the position of the contemporary "pluralism" school of missiology. He contrasts these to a "dialogical relationship." See *The Dialogical Imperative: A Christian Reflection on Interfaith Encounter* (1991:5-26).

6. Some hold that this approach was a mistake and that Paul changed his approach thereafter, but there is no hint of criticism by Luke or mention of such a change. This notion is based upon the interpretation of 1 Corinthians 1:18ff. as a rejection of the Athens approach. There is no textual basis for such a connection.

7. Leonard Swidler's ten rules for dialogue, with the exception of number 10 which states that "each participant eventually must attempt to experience the partner's religion or ideology 'from within,' " are a helpful guide to what Howard Netland calls "formal dialogue." They emphasize fairness, honesty and sincerity, speaking "for oneself," not bringing to the conversation "hard and fast assumptions" about the partner, and a willingness to be self-critical. See *Toward a Universal Theology of Religion* (1987:14-16).

Bibliography

Abrams, Ray
  1969   *Preachers Present Arms*. Scottdale: Herald Press.

Azevendo, Marcello deC.
  1987   *Basic Ecclesial Communities in Brazil: The Challenge of a New Way of Being Church*. Washington, D.C.: Georgetown University Press.

Babbage, Stuart Barton
  1957   *Man in Nature and in Grace*. Grand Rapids: Eerdmans.

Baillie, Donald
  1948   *God Was in Christ*. New York: Scribners.

Banks, Robert
  1980   *Paul's Idea of Community: The Early House Churches in Their Historical Setting*. Grand Rapids: Eerdmans.

Barna, George
  1991   *What Americans Believe*. Ventura, Calif.: Regal Books.

Barnett, Maurice
  1953   *The Living Flame*. London: Epworth Press.

Bellah, Robert, et al.
  1985   *Habits of the Heart: Individualism and Commitment in American Life*. New York: Harper & Row.

Boers, Arthur Paul
  1991   *On Earth As in Heaven*. Scottdale: Herald Press.

Bornkamm, Heinrich
  1965   *Luther's World of Thought*. St. Louis: Concordia.

Bowman, J. W.
  1959   "The Term 'Gospel' and Its Cognates in the Palestinian Syriac," in *New Testament Essays: Studies in Memory of T. W. Manson (1893-*

1958), edited by A. J. B. Higgins. Manchester: Manchester University Press.

Brown, Raymond E.
1979 *The Community of the Beloved Disciple*. New York/ Ramsey: Paulist Press.
1984 *The Churches the Apostles Left Behind*. New York/ Ramsey: Paulist Press.

Bruce, F. F.
1954 *The Book of Acts*. Grand Rapids: Eerdmans.

Bruner, F. D.
1970 *A Theology of the Holy Spirit*. Grand Rapids: Eerdmans.

Capra, Fritjof
1983 *The Turning Point*. Toronto/New York: Bantam Books.

Chafer, L. S.
1948 *Systematic Theology, Volume VII*. Dallas: Dallas Seminary.

Chandler, Russell
1988 *Understanding the New Age*. Waco, Tex.: Word.

Cullmann, Oscar
1962 *Peter: Disciple, Apostle, Martyr*. Philadelphia: Westminster Press.

Cullmann, Oscar
1967 *Salvation in History*. New York: Harper & Row.

Denny, James
1976 *Studies in Theology*. (Reprint of 1895 edition.) Grand Rapids: Baker Book House.

Doi, Takeo
1973 *The Anatomy of Dependence*. New York: Harper & Row.

Eichrodt, Walther
1951 *Man in the Old Testament*. Naperville, Ill.: Alec R. Alleson.

Flew, R. Newton
1943 *Jesus and His Church: A Study of the Idea of the Ecclesia in the New Testament* (2nd. ed.). London: Epworth Press.

Freyne, Sean
1980 *The World of the New Testament*. Michael Glazier: Wilmington, Del.

Fridrichsen, Anton (ed.)
  1953   *The Root of the Vine*. New York: Philosophical Library.

Friedrich, Gerhard
  1964   "Euangelion," *Theological Dictionary of the New Testament*, vol. 2,
          ed. by Gerhard Kittle. Grand Rapids: Eerdmans.

Garrett, James Leo (ed.)
  1969   *The Concept of the Believers' Church*. Scottdale: Herald Press.

Gilkey, Langdon
  1964   *How the Church Can Minister to the World Without Losing Itself*. New
          York: Harper & Row.

Groothuis, Douglas R.
  1986   *Unmasking the New Age*. Downers Grove, Ill.: InterVarsity Press.

Handy, Robert T.
  1971   *A Christian America: Protestant Hopes and Historical Realities*. New
          York: Oxford.

Harrison, Everett F.
  1985   *The Apostolic Church*. Grand Rapids: Eerdmans.

Haselden, Kyle
  1959   *The Racial Problem in Christian Perspective*. New York: Harper &
          Row.

Hengel, Martin
  1983   *Between Jesus and Paul*. Philadelphia: Fortress Press.
  1985   *Studies in the Gospel of Mark*. Philadelphia: Fortress Press.

Hull, J. H. E.
  1967   *The Holy Spirit in the Acts of the Apostles*. London: Lutterworth.

Hunter, A. M.
  1944   *The Message of the New Testament*. Philadelphia: Westminster
          Press.
  1953   *A Pattern for Life*. Philadelphia: Westminster Press.

Kee, Howard, Franklin Young, and Karlfried Froelich
  1965   *Understanding the New Testament*. Englewood Cliffs: Prentice Hall.

Kingsbury, Jack Dean
  1986   *Proclamation Commentaries: Matthew* (second edition). Philadel-
          phia: Fortress Press.

Kittel, Gerhard (ed.)
   1965   *Theological Dictionary of the New Testament*, Volume III. Grand Rapids: Eerdmans.

Klassen, William
   1966   *The Forgiving Community*. Philadelphia: Westminster Press.

Klassen, William and Graydon Snyder (eds.)
   1962   *Current Issues in New Testament Interpretation*. New York: Harper.

Kraus, C. Norman
   1958   *Dispensationalism in American: Its Rise and Development*. Richmond, Va.: John Knox.
   1972   *The Healing Christ*. Scottdale: Herald Press.
   1990   *Jesus Christ Our Lord. Christology from a Disciple's Perspective*. Scottdale: Herald Press.

Kraybill, Donald
   1990   *The Upside-Down Kingdom*. Scottdale: Herald Press.

Ladd, George Eldon
   1971   *The Gospel of the Kingdom*. Grand Rapids: Eerdmans.

Lampe, G. W. H.
   1955 "The Holy Spirit in the Writings of St. Luke," in *Studies in the Gospels*, ed. by D. E. Nineham. Oxford: Oxford University Press.

Lewis, C. S.
   1960   *Four Loves*. New York: Harcourt Brace Jovanovich.

Littell, Franklin
   1961   *A Tribute to Menno*. Scottdale: Herald Press.

Lohfink, Gerhard
   1984   *Jesus and Community: The Social Dimension of Christian Faith*. Philadelphia: Fortress Press, and New York: Paulist Press.

Macgregor, G. H. C.
   1929   *The Gospel of John, The Moffatt Commentary*. New York: Harper Brothers.

Manson, T. W.
   1963   *The Teaching of Jesus*. Cambridge: University Press.

Mays, James Luther (ed.)
   1987   *Interpreting the Gospels*. Philadelphia: Fortress Press.

McNeill, John T. (ed.)
   1960   *Calvin: Institutes of the Christian Religion*. Philadelphia: Westminster Press.

Mead, Sidney
   1963   *The Lively Experiment, The Shaping of Christianity in America*. New York: Harper & Row.

Meeks, Wayne A.
   1983   *The First Urban Christians: The Social World of the Apostle Paul*. New Haven and London: Yale.

Mendenhall, G. E.
   1960   "The Relation of the Individual to Political Society in Ancient Israel," *Biblical Studies in Memory of H. C. Alleman*, J. M. Myers, editor. Locust Valley, N.Y.: J. J. Augustin Publishers.

Morris, Leon
         The Gospel According to John (The New International Commentary of the New Testament). Grand Rapids: Eerdmans.

Moule, C. F. D.
   1965   *The Gospel According to Mark.* (The Cambridge Bible Commentary on the N.E.B.) Cambridge: University Press.

Myers, J. M. (ed.)
   1960   *Biblical Studies in Memory of H. C. Alleman*. Locust Valley, N.Y.: J. J. Augustin Publishers.

Netland, Howard
   1991   *The Dialogical Imperative: A Christian Reflection on Interfaith Encounter*. Grand Rapids: Eerdmans.

Nicholls, Bruce J. (ed.)
   1968   *The Church God's Agent for Change.* Grand Rapids: Baker/Paternoster Press.

Niebuhr, H. Richard
   1951   *Christ and Culture*. New York: Harper.

Nineham, D. E. (ed.)
   1955   *Studies in the Gospels*. New York: Oxford.

Phipps, William E.
   1973   "The Sensuousness of Agape," *Theology Today*, (January, pp. 370-379).

Piper, Otto
   1953   "Exodus in the New Testament," *Interpretation* (January, pp. 3-22).

Porter, J. R.
   1965   "The Legal Aspects of the Concept of 'Corporate Personality' in the Old Testament," *Vetus Testamentum*, XI (July).

Robinson, H. Wheeler
   1928/1958 *The Christian Experience of the Holy Spirit*. London: Nisbet, and New York: Harper Press.
   1935/1964 *Corporate Personality in Ancient Israel*, Facet Book. Philadelphia: Fortress.

Rogerson, J. W.
   1970   "The Hebrew Conception of Corporate Personality: A Reexamination," *Journal of Theological Studies*, XXI (April).

Rowden, Harold H.
   1967   *The Origins of the Brethren, 1825-1850*. London: Pickering and Inglis.

Sandeen, Ernest R.
   1970   *The Roots of Fundamentalism, British and American Millenarianism 1800-1930*. Chicago: University of Chicago.

Schanz, John P.
   1977   *A Theology of Community*. Washington, D.C.: University Press of America.

Schnackenburg, Rudolf
   1990   *The Gospel According to St. John*, Volume III. New York: Crossroads.
   1965   *The Church in the New Testament*. New York: Seabury Press, and Herder K. G.

Scott, E. F.
   1947   *Man and Society in the New Testament.* New York: Scribners.

Scriven, Charles
   1988   *The Transformation of Culture: Christian Social Ethics After H. Richard Niebuhr*. Scottdale: Herald Press

Shedd, Russel
   1964   *Man in Community*. Grand Rapids: Eerdmans.

Shibley, David
    1989   *A Force in the Earth, The Charismatic Renewal and World Evangelism.*
            Altamonte Springs, Fla.: Creation House.

Sider, Ronald E.
    1979   *Christ and Violence.* Scottdale: Herald Press.

Skinner, B. F.
    1971   *Beyond Freedom and Dignity.* New York: Knopf.

Snyder, Howard
    1977   *The Community of the King.* Downers Grove: InterVarsity Press.

Starkey, Lycurgus M.
    1962   *The Work of the Holy Spirit: A Study in Wesleyan Theology.* New York
            & Nashville: Abingdon.

Stendahl, Krister
    1963   "The Apostle Paul and the Introspective Conscience of the
            West," *Harvard Theological Review* 1963 (202ff.).

Stoeffler, Ernest
    1965   *The Rise of Evangelical Pietism.* Leiden: E. J. Brill.

Swidler, Leonard (ed.)
    1987   *Toward a Universal Theology of Religion.* Maryknoll, N.Y.: Orbis.

Synan, Vinson
    1971   *The Holiness Pentecostal Movement.* Grand Rapids: Eerdmans.

Taylor, John V.
    1963   *The Primal Vision.* London: S. C. M. Press.

Tinsley, E. J.
    1965   *The Gospel According to Luke.* (The Cambridge Bible Commentary
            of the NEB) Cambridge: University Press.

Trocmé, André
    1974   *Jesus and the Nonviolent Revolution.* Scottdale: Herald Press.

Verkuyl, J.
    1978   *Contemporary Missiology.* Grand Rapids: Eerdmans.

Wagner, C. Peter
    1986   *Spiritual Power and Church Growth.* Altamonte Springs, Fla.: Cre-
            ation House.

Wahlstrom, Eric
   1950   *The New Life in Christ*. Philadelphia: Muhlenberg.

Warfield, B. B.
   1953   *Miracles: Yesterday and Today, True and False*. Grand Rapids: Eerdmans.

Watson, David
   1978   *I Believe in the Church*. Grand Rapids: Eerdmans.

Weaver, Dorthy Jean
   1990   *The Missionary Discourse in the Gospel of Matthew: A Literary Critical Analysis*. Sheffield, England: JSOT.

Welch, Claude
   1958   *The Reality of the Church*. New York: Scribners.

Wenger, John C. (ed.)
   1956   *The Complete Works of Menno Simons*. Scottdale: Herald Press.

Westerhoff III, John H.
   1985   *Living the Faith Community: The Church That Makes a Difference*. Minneapolis, Minn.: Winston Press.

Williams, Colin
   1963   *Where in the World?* New York: N. C. C.
   1964   *What in the World?* New York: N. C. C.

Williams, Rodman
   1972   *The Pentecostal Reality*. Waco, Tex.: Logos International.

Wink, Walter
   1987   *Violence and Nonviolence in South Africa: Jesus' Third Way*. Philadelphia: New Society Publishers.

Wright, George Ernest
   1954   *The Biblical Doctrine of Man in Society.* London: S.C.M. Press.

Yoder, John Howard
   1972   *The Politics of Jesus*. Grand Rapids: Eerdmans.

Scripture Index

Subject Index

The Author

C. Norman Kraus is a teacher-missionary, now retired, who served at Goshen College and Seminary (Elkhart, Indiana) and with Mennonite Board of Missions. He has been a lecturer, author, and activist. He represents the Mennonite Church to the Mennonite Central Committee Board and serves as its theological and spiritual consultant.

As his writings illustrate, Kraus has devoted his life to the Mennonite Church as a scholar interested not only in academic and theological issues but also in the body life and witness of the church in the world. While a teacher at Goshen College, he founded the Center for Discipleship to encourage students to study issues of social ethics and witness. He was concerned for the church's role in the civil rights movement and was personally involved in the movement during the 1950s and 1960s. He helped begin a new type of congregation, called the Assembly, which emphasized life and witness together in "Koinonia" groups.

In 1979 Kraus and his wife, Ruth, accepted an assignment from the Mennonite Board of Missions to go to Japan. There they worked with the young Mennonite churches of Hokkaido as teacher-consultants in the emerging fellowships. While there, Kraus wrote the first volume of his theology, *Jesus Christ Our Lord*, published simultaneously in Japan and the United States.

He earned college degrees from both Eastern Mennonite College and Goshen College. He received a B.D. from Goshen Biblical Seminary, a Th.M. from Princeton Theological Seminary, and in 1961 a Ph.D. from Duke University.

Kraus has had published many journal articles and has written, edited, or contributed to numerous books. Among recent books are *Jesus Christ Our Lord* (Herald Press, 1987, 1990) and *God Our Savior* (Herald Press, 1991).

Kraus was born in Denbigh (now Newport News) Virginia. He was married to Ruth Smith in 1945, and they raised five children. He and Ruth now live in Harrisonburg, Virginia, where they continue to be active in the local Mennonite conference and congregations.